Writing
is not Magic,
it's Design

T0382225

BIS Publishers

Borneostraat 80-A
1094 CP Amsterdam
The Netherlands

T +31 (0)20 515 02 30

bis@bispublishers.com
www.bispublishers.com
ISBN 978 90 636 9697 9

Book design by Raquel Guerreiro

Writing is not Magic, it's Design

The designer's guide to writing
and supercharging creativity

João Batalheiro Ferreira

BIS Publishers

Contents

"I write entirely to find out what I'm thinking, what I'm looking at, what I see and what it means."

Joan Didion

"It's not the writing part that's hard. What's hard is sitting down to write."

Steven Pressfield

Introduction
A writing method for designers

Writing is intimidating, I get it. As designers, we spend our time developing ideas with visuals, not words. For us, writing is an afterthought, a chore we postpone, or a task we run away from and avoid. But what happens when you can't avoid it? When you must write something long and complex like a dissertation? Or when you strive to get a journaling habit going? Then, you struggle and suffer and succumb to procrastination. But you don't have to.

Designers often say they can't write because they're a "visual person". This is nonsense. You were not wired at birth to think in a certain way. The brain is a fantastically malleable organ. You can be a designer *and* be able to write, too. Just think of the written contributions of designers like Paul Rand, Paula Scher, Michael Bierut, Ellen Lupton, Manuel Lima, or Per Mollerup.

Forget about writing as the obscure art of a literary few. Anybody can write because writing is a skill. Like any other skill, you improve by learning the basics and practising. And the first step is changing how you think about writing.

Writing is a communication problem, not a set of conventions to follow. It's not about grammar or punctuation any more than architecture is about bricks. Writing is about ideas. The goal of writing is to **communicate ideas to other people using words**. This is true of a song lyric, a poem, an essay, a newsletter, a love letter, an article, a blog post, a piece of copy, a dissertation, a novel, or a nonfiction book. Writing is about reaching someone else's mind, and sometimes their heart as well.

This is far less intimidating. Designers communicate ideas to other people all the time: A logo is designed to communicate a brand's identity, an ATM interface communicates the list of possible actions, and the shape of a door handle communicates if you should *push* or *pull*. Your design fails if people can't understand it. Writing also fails if it doesn't communicate clearly.

But here's the good news: if you learn to write with clarity and precision, a host of benefits follow like a cognitive army reinforcing your mental arsenal. To communicate ideas, you must first understand them deeply. Like Bob Dylan said: "I'll know my song well before I start singing." So, to reach other people's minds, we must first dive into our own.

Writing opens a door into the landscape of our thoughts. Finding the right words to express an idea means we must think the idea through. It doesn't matter if you're writing an academic paper, advertising copy, a diary entry, or a newsletter. If you can't explain something using words, you don't really understand it. And articulating an idea with words is part of understanding it. Writing and thinking are so entangled we don't know what comes first: the words or the thoughts.

About the book

Now that I have your attention, here's the deal:

I have been helping designers learn how to write for years, and I assure you anyone can do it. This book won't bag you a Nobel or a Pulitzer prize,* but it's not aiming for that. What it promises is straightforward: a practical writing method tailored for designers. The book offers advice to tackle any writing assignment or personal project. It won't delve into grammar conventions nor offer tips for ad copy, academia, or social media posts. The conventions of specific industries change, but good writing principles endure.

The book presents a four-step writing method created to align with how designers think. These steps guide you through the **mechanics** of writing: how to gather insights, combine ideas, master the building blocks of writing, and produce clear and precise prose that reaches other people. The book equips you with skills that grow into good writing habits, including:

- A complete method to manage the writing process from early ideas to polished prose;
- Techniques to overcome blank-page anxiety (or 'writer's block');
- How to connect ideas to generate new insights;
- Master the building blocks of writing: the *sentence* and the *paragraph*;
- How to edit your writing for clarity and precision.

* *If it does, please let me know about it*

Writing is a process you can learn, not a talent you're born with. It's not magic, it's design. You don't have to take my word for it; here's how Steven Pinker, a renowned cognitive psychologist and language expert, describes writing:

A coherent text is a designed object (...) like other designed objects, it comes about not by accident but by drafting a blueprint, attending to details and maintaining a sense of harmony and balance.

Let me put it another way: writing does not emerge in sudden bursts of literary inspiration; a text is carefully constructed with a purpose. You put it together piece by piece until it works. Learn how to craft a sentence and construct a paragraph, and you have the building blocks of writing at your disposal.

Writing is a craft you can master, like cooking or playing the piano. While the product of writing is impressive, each part of the writing process is remarkably simple. If you know how the parts stack up, the result may look like magic, but the process is anything but.

Read on if you want to develop an extra skill. Writing helps you learn faster, generate insights, and deepen your ideas. A designer who doesn't write has a creative disadvantage, like a race car driver unable to shift into sixth gear. Writing is the mechanism that shifts your thinking into sixth gear. This book shows you how.

Writing Process

The blank page

You sit down to write. The sun is up, the coffee is brewed and steaming on your desk, you face the empty page on the screen. The cursor blinks in a stubborn rhythm, you notice it matches your heartbeat. Or is it the other way around? You write a sentence. Then you rewrite it, rearrange the words, change a verb. It's not quite there yet. The coffee is cold, you start again. You write a sentence, it sounds good! You move on to the next sentence but notice a repeated word, so you return to the first sentence and adjust it. It's lunchtime.

Sounds familiar? I see it all the time with my design students. Like most people who don't write for a living, designers fall into the perfect sentence trap: a cycle of writing and rewriting the same thing until they either give up or put it off to tomorrow. And who can blame them? Writing like this is like riding a bicycle while holding the brakes: slow, painful, and you arrive nowhere. No wonder most people put off writing until they are pinned down to the desk by a forceful deadline.

Imagine you're designing a chair. On day one of the project, you start building a final prototype and technical drawings to send out for production. Ridiculous, right? You can't just bypass the design process and begin at the end. When you start a project, you're not concerned with how perfect your design is. Most designers I know start by drawing tiny sketches on their notebooks, sometimes on a napkin. They don't worry about quality because these sketches are not for show.

They're for thinking. Then, as an idea grows, you gradually work out the details until you settle on a finished piece.

Why would writing be different? Writing is also a gradual process with different stages. And different stages call for different *types of writing*. There is a time to obsess over the right verb. That time is not day one. Writing involves gathering information, writing personal notes, working out a tentative outline, putting together a rough first draft, and editing it. Now, notice how similar it is to designing:

STAGES	WRITING	DESIGNING
1	Gather information	Gather information
2	Take notes	Sketch
3	Outline	Design specifications
4	Draft	Model
5	Edit	Prototype

We could add a sixth stage for user testing/ask a friend to read your text for feedback. The writing/designing parallelism is unsurprising. Design and writing are creative efforts, and creativity is a universal human trait. Architects, journalists, and even scientists roughly follow the same basic steps from making sense of a problem to creating something new, whether it's a building, an article, or a theory.

Writing, like designing, is gradual: no matter how long or short your text is, you must follow specific steps, and each of those steps belongs to a stage of the writing process.

Writing requires you to gather information and think, take note of your insights, shape your material, and polish it. Both novices and professional writers follow these stages, but a novice follows them **for every sentence**, which is mentally impossible to sustain for more than five minutes. That's why novices are easy prey for the perfect sentence trap. And procrastination.

An experienced writer, on the contrary, works in smaller sections. As a designer, I like to think about these sections as *modules*.

Modular writing

A module is an independent unit that can be combined with other independent units to build a larger whole. Modules are indivisible pieces, like Lego blocks. Legos are simple building blocks you can arrange to create complex structures. With modular building blocks, complexity emerges from simplicity. We see it in nature, where atoms are shaped into every life form. In writing, the smallest building blocks are *sentences*; we will deal with them in Part III.

Atoms, Lego bricks, and sentences are modular building blocks. Pieces you assemble to create something new. But modules can also be larger units with specific functions. For instance, in the automotive industry, the same engine can fit into distinct car models. In programming, engineers reuse code snippets with specific functions across different software applications. Modern furniture is modular, too; you can assemble a bookcase with shelves that fit vinyl records or smaller ones that fit paperbacks.

In writing, a module is a text that stands on its own. It's a written piece you understand even without reading what preceded it. The chapter you're reading is a module; it makes sense on its own and expresses a specific point. It logically follows from what came before and connects with what comes next, but it can also be read in isolation. It has a clear beginning, middle, and end. And it makes a self-contained point.

A writing assignment is a shapeless thing. At best, it's a statement of intentions: "I want to write a *book*," "I have to finish the *report* by Wednesday," or "I really need to start working on my *dissertation*." The book, the report, and the dissertation are just goals. Vague intentions you plan to complete someday when you carve out time from your busy schedule. But vague goals are the grounds where procrastination pitches its tent.

Procrastination is a powerful force because it leverages psychological frailties. People don't give up on their goals. It's much easier to postpone them for tomorrow. We rarely say, "I give up;" we say, "I'll do it tomorrow." Leaving it for tomorrow is balm on a wound, it means we never really deal with the problem. We never do the work nor give up. We postpone it.

Author Steven Pressfield calls it *resistance*. In his book "The War of Art," Pressfield describes resistance as an invisible force that opposes creative efforts, personal growth, or any positive change in our lives. It is the force that prevents us from doing the work we know we should do, pursuing our passions, or achieving our goals.

Resistance is universal, everybody struggles with it. Novices struggle harder because they don't know how to deal with it. They lack the tools to tackle a writing assignment effectively. A novice writer faces a writing assignment like someone standing at the bottom of a mountain, wondering how to reach the top without gear our climbing experience.

I've noticed this problem in designers. At the root of the issue, we find the wrong perspective. Novice writers think of writing as one large thing (a mountain), a single activity where you move from a blank page to a polished piece of prose, from the bottom to the top, following a linear sequence. Experienced writers, on the contrary, know they must break a writing assignment down into smaller parts, or the task never takes shape.

The first step to overcoming resistance involves changing how you think about the writing process. Writing doesn't move sequentially from a blank page to a finished written piece, any more than you design a chair in one go. There are different parts to a design and different stages in the design process. It's the same with writing.

Adopting a modular approach is a good technique to manage the writing process. You write in smaller meaningful units that fit together into a completed whole. A writing assignment may be large or small, but you must always break it down into sections you can manage. Nobody can write a whole book. That's impossible. But anyone can put together a rough draft of the first chapter. The same is true for a post, an essay, or a report. You must find smaller meaningful units (your modules), work on each one separately, and figure out how to assemble them later.

Writing in smaller sections is more human, manageable, and fun: Instead of an oppressive blank page, you identify smaller goals you can achieve. The menacing assignment shrinks like a dragon transformed into many tiny, harmless lizards.

Always break down a writing assignment into smaller modules you can tackle individually. Even a short post can be separated into three paragraphs, each making a self-contained point.

Modular assembly

A piece of writing is *assembled.*

Novices view the writing process like the linear assembly line of a 20th Century factory. In a car factory, the conveyor belt assembly is one long manufacturing process that moves linearly from start to finish. Initially, the frame takes shape, slowly moving down the line. As it progresses, workers add parts—engines, wheels, and doors. Until a fully assembled car rolls off the line

The conveyor belt is a metaphor for how novices write. They start with a blank page and slowly build a text from the beginning, moving towards development, and finishing with the conclusion. This seems reasonable. As readers, we experience reading as a sequence that follows the beginning, middle, and end structure. The problem is that how we *read* a text and how we *write* a text are radically different things.

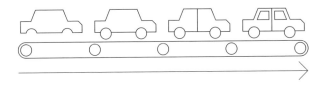

Reading and writing

Reading and writing involve several contrasts and key differences:

1. Linear vs. Modular

Reading: Readers follow a linear progression through a text, starting from the beginning and moving through the middle to reach the end.

Writing: Writers, on the other hand, approach their work modularly. They jump between section drafts, edit various parts, or start sections before finishing others. The writing process is flexible and non-linear.

2.   Immediate Understanding vs. Gradual Construction

Reading: Readers understand a text step by step, grasping the content as it unfolds; they follow a logical flow that makes sense from start to finish.

Writing: Writers gradually construct their work, piecing together ideas, refining sentences, and revising content over time. Sometimes, a writer only makes complete sense of his own work towards the end of the writing process.

3.   Fixed Text vs. Evolving Drafts

Reading: Readers engage with a fixed, completed text. They see the finished product, with the structure and content already determined.

Writing: Writers work with evolving drafts. A text is subject to constant revision, with multiple iterations before reaching a final version. The process is dynamic and ongoing.

A final text does not reflect the nature of its writing process. It's the opposite. Readers experience a text as a linear whole, a neat progression from beginning to end. The writer, on the other hand, experiences the text as an evolving piece with multiple iterations. For a writer, writing a text and discovering what it means is the same process. A text evolves piece by piece, and the sequence of the pieces is found near the end when it finally makes sense.

The writing process is nothing like a linear assembly line, it's more like directing a film.

Directing a film

When we watch a film, we experience it with a clear beginning, middle, and end.* But we've all watched enough making-of documentaries to know that that is not how movies are made. The filming crew may shoot a scene from the third act in the morning and a scene from the middle of the story in the afternoon. After eight or nine weeks of filming, the director holds hours upon hours of different takes from multiple scenes.

The film is shaped in the *editing* room, where the director arranges the scenes into a sequence. Writing is the same.

We manage the writing process like a director making a film. We tackle each scene one by one and figure out the sequence in the editing room.** In writing, instead of a linear assembly line, you have a modular assembly process.

In a modular assembly, independent processes construct parts that fit together as a whole. Each module is independently created, developed, and edited, like shooting scenes for a film.

For example, imagine you want to write a short presentation for a chair you designed. You want something short and snappy to use in a press release, a newsletter, and social media posts.

---

*   I'm aware some films challenge conventional narrative structures; that makes them the exception, not the rule.

**   The film script, of course, functions as the *outline*, more on Part II.

Three aspects make your chair unique: it's stackable, it was manufactured locally, and made with sustainable bioplastics.

But you're unsure how to begin. Perhaps open with a story about how personal the project is for you. Or start by acknowledging a classic chair design that influenced you? But you feel uninspired, blank-page anxiety sets in, and you put it off to tomorrow.

Luckily, you read this book. You know you don't have to start writing from the beginning. You already have your three modules: the chair is stackable, manufactured locally, and made with sustainable bioplastics. You write each part independently without bothering with perfection. You put down the material into a first draft. The result? Instead of a blank page tormenting you, you now have something to work with.

You make three decent points, but notice it sounds too technical. So, you balance the text with a personal observation, a story, or a particular detail about the chair. Now you have a good introduction, something human the reader can relate with. You conclude with a nod to the people who will use it.

That's it. When writing, it doesn't matter where you begin because you write each part independently and later connect the parts to form a whole.

The principle of modular writing holds regardless of how long or short your text is. Whether it's a PhD thesis, a blog post, or a press release, it would be madness to begin with a blank page and move from an introduction to a conclusion in a conveyor belt-like process. That leads to the perfect sentence trap and blank page anxiety.

The writing process is modular. You break up the text into parts, construct them independently, and assemble them. Sometimes, I have no idea where to begin a text, but I know how I want it to end. When that happens, instead of struggling for ages with the beginning, I write the ending first and spend the rest of the time working on a story that leads to it.

In short

1.   Break your writing assignment into sections; these are your modules.

2.   Each module can be written independently, because each one makes a coherent and self-contained point, and has a beginning, middle, and end.

3.   After writting the modules, you assemble them in a sequence, like a director piecing together scenes for a film.

A modular approach is the first part of getting the writing process under control. The second part is mastering the **writing stages**.

The four stages of writing

Writing, much like designing, is not one large uniform activity.

If a friend asks what you did yesterday, it would be strange to answer "I spent the afternoon designing" because "designing" is too broad and ambiguous. Instead, you might say, "Yesterday I worked on a prototype," "I gathered visual references for the book cover," or "I tested fonts for the app we've been working on." Depending on where you are in the design process, you'll be doing different types of designing. Writing is similar.

Writing involves different activities, each playing a different role in the writing process. When we break the writing process down, we get:

NODE
Note – Outline – Draft – Edit

These are the four stages of writing. The stages are connected, and you may go back and forth between them, but the writing process is linear. In other words, you can't *outline* before you gathered enough *notes*; it's much harder to *draft* without an outline and you definitely cannot *edit* before you have a draft, just like you can't sculpt without a piece of marble.

When you divide it into these stages, the writing process becomes so simple it can be explained in a few sentences: First, you gather information by taking notes. Then, you sort the notes into topics and arrange them in a sequence, which is the outline of your text. Take your notes for each topic and paste them into a separate document; that's your rough draft. Finally, you edit the draft into a finished piece.

None of the four steps described above are particularly hard. So why do most people find writing so difficult? Because they do all the steps at once.* But each stage of writing covers a range of activities that require a different mindset.

The NODE stages of writing

STAGES	PURPOSE	ACTIVITIES	MINDSET
Note	Gather information	Read, reflect, research, connect, observe, notice	Curiosity, mind-wandering, associative
Outline	Get an overview	Structure, organise, visualise	Visual, analytical
Draft	First version	Compose, generate, elaborate	Nonjudgemental
Edit	Polish	Sculpt, cut, arrange, correct	Focus, craftsmanship

* *See the blank page chapter*

As you can see, each writing stage requires a particular kind of mindset. It's easy to understand why. If you're like me, you may find it hard to focus *and* let your mind wander at the same time. Also, different daytimes are more conducive to different mindsets. You may realise that you're better at editing in the evenings or enjoy reviewing your notes in the morning. Each person discovers their ideal daytime for each writing stage.

A Writing Method

The NODE stages and the modular approach to writing work together as a writing method:

1. Break any writing assignment into smaller parts you can manage. Each part should tackle a single point or cover one topic or theme; these parts are *modules* because they can be written independently and make sense for the reader. The writing modules form a coherent unit of text, which means that later they can be moved into different sequences with minimal editing.

2. Follow the Note, Outline, Draft, and Edit writing stages when working on each module. This allows you to concentrate all your mental energy on each point without becoming overwhelmed with the task.

NODE Example

Scenario: you're tasked with writing a piece about how your studio uses *design thinking* in its working process. The piece will be published in the studio's newsletter, social media pages, and blog section of their homepage.

It's not a huge assignment, but it's complicated enough to scare you into procrastinating. Let's see how it looks if we apply a modular writing approach.

Design Thinking is a broad topic. So, we break it down into manageable sections: (1) *What is Design Thinking* and (2) *How do we apply it?* These topics are still broad, but we begin to make sense of the assignment by breaking it down into parts. Now you can look into design thinking as a topic and research some of its history; at the same time, you can perhaps gather some information about an excellent example of design thinking from your studio.

1. What is Design Thinking?
M1 Definition
M2 History

2. How do we apply it?
M3 Quotes from the senior designers
M4 Example of real-life project

Now you have four smaller modules you can tackle individually. You can begin by reading articles or books about design thinking and taking notes on material you can use for your piece. At the same time, you can gather quotes from senior colleagues about a particular case they remember from a project. Then, create separate documents for each writing module and paste all your content (your notes) into them. The blank page is no longer empt.

You build on your notes to draft each separate module. It doesn't matter where you start because the final sequence is not clear yet. Expand on your notes, and write each part separately until it makes sense on its own.

Now, you take your four parts and figure out an outline for the piece. Don't worry, it's not set in stone:

- Introduction about design thinking
- M1 Define and explain it
- M2 Short outline of its history
- M3 Describe an example of design thinking
- M4 Add details, quotes, or interesting stories you gathered
- Snappy conclusion

You get a first draft when you combine separate documents into a single piece. Slowly, your finished piece starts to come together. Now, read it and see if it flows. Give it to someone else and ask for feedback. If the sequence doesn't work, you can change it, cut parts, or edit others; the process is iterative.

The modular approach turns vague assignments into smaller pieces you can tackle. This way, you don't have to procrastinate and wait until the final moment before a deadline to write the whole thing in one stress-inducing session. You don't have to dread starting because the effort is progressive. It begins with humble note-taking. You never start writing before you research and gather notes. The writing process depends on your note-taking; you can't outline, draft, or edit without first taking notes.

This may sound too pragmatic. Is there no place for the genius dictating complete masterpieces from mind to paper? Well, that romantic ideal may be useful for a Hollywood biopic about Hemingway, but it's useless in the real world of people and their deadlines. Novelists and other writing geniuses are the wrong model to follow. A better writing model for a designer (whether a student, researcher, or professional) is the journalist.

A writing model

Journalists are good models because they don't write to express themselves artistically; they write to tell a story. They gather information, distinguish the essential from the irrelevant, build a narrative that ties it together, and craft a finished piece that carries a punch without wasting any words. When battling for the expensive real estate of newspaper or magazine pages, word count matters. In good writing, like good design, *less is more.*

The NODE method of writing is inspired by how seasoned journalists work. The method is simple because a good method removes complexity. A method does not add options or depend on complex tools that clutter your workflow. All you need is a sharp mind and a reliable writing system. The rest is whatever works for you. It is irrelevant whether you write on a computer or longhand, using sophisticated software or post-its, Microsoft Word or a pencil.

The NODE method improves how you write, and after a while, it will improve how you *think*. Mastering a skill deepens your perception of the world. Any musician can tell you that learning how to play an instrument rewires your brain (for the better). So does mastering how to write.

You're about to take the first step into a larger world. And it begins with the note.

Part II

Writing Method

Note

Outline

Draft

Edit

If you can
look, see.
If you can
see, notice.

José Saramago

Note

Let's return to that blank page. Most people struggle with writing because they believe the process starts with an empty page. Now, if you have nothing to fill the page with, you have good reason to struggle. You stare and you strive and you write a few tentative lines, but eventually writing seems as impossible as bending a spoon with your mind.

Do not try to fill an empty page, that's impossible. Instead, realise the truth: there is no blank page, only insufficient notes.*

Of course, taking notes may seem trivial, any teenage student can scribble a few notes during his classes. But while it's true that notes are *simple*, they are definitely not trivial.

Notes are written records that serve as memory aids. But *to note* is also a verb that means to notice or pay attention to something: you notice your son is unusually quiet, a melodic piano run buried in an otherwise ordinary pop song, or a change in the weather before rainfall. A note is always associated with a shift in attention. First you notice something, then you note it down.

Notes are also a tool to make sense of information. For instance, when you read a book, you run through multiple pages of facts, stories, events and other information. When you're done, you forget most of it. If asked, you describe the gist of the book but ignore the details.

---

*   *For readers born after the year 2000, I'm referencing The Matrix movie.*

We couldn't live without this capacity to discriminate between information coming our way. Walking down the street would take forever if you paid equal attention to all the conversations around you, the sound of every car driving by, every ad on every billboard, every leaf on every tree; you get the picture.

We choose what matters and what doesn't. When reading, 300 pages may boil down to a couple of underlined passages and three or four notes scribbled on the margins. These notes are altogether personal. After all, different people reading the same book will notice different things. What matters is a matter of personal choice.

Our notes follow a particular way of seeing the world, so notes are an extension of ourselves. If you develop a method to consistently write notes on all you read, listen to, watch, and everything else you experience, you'll build an invaluable collection of observations about the things that resonate with you. A unique collection of what captured your attention.

You always have somewhere to start when you hold a collection of personal observations. The dreaded blank page never shows up because you begin with your notes. What's more, your writing won't sound like a bland Wikipedia article. Instead, it will be alive with your point of view. Writing will be the unique product of your mind.

The Noticing Mind

Notes have three key qualities: (1) They result from a shift in your attention, which makes them deeply **personal**. (2) Notes make sense of information and help you decide what's **meaningful**. (3) Notes have the quality of **enduring**. They are not useful for a specific project and then archived, discarded, or forgotten; instead, if you store your notes effectively, like faithful friends, they appear when needed.

Three key qualities of notes
- Personal
- Meaningful
- Enduring

Note-taking transcends what a teenager does during class. At a basic level, notes are memory aids, but at a higher level, they support your thinking process: Much like a sketch, a note is a temporary holder of a hazy thought. By externalising what you're thinking, you can literally *look at* your idea and analyse it. Let's say you're trying to understand a difficult passage in a book; a quick note using your own words will test whether you understood it.

The mind depends upon external support to reason. That's why designers sketch during the design process; they sketch to think. Notes are similar to sketches in that they help you think through problems (and solutions). Likewise, a note is often our first attempt at making sense of a topic or a rough outline of an idea.

But notes are also powerful because while sketches help during a particular project, notes grow and stay with you forever. For example, I have a note on something Steve Jobs said during an interview: "Design is how it works." I've used

The power
of the unaided
mind is highly
overrated.
Without
external aids,
deep, sustained
reasoning
is difficult.

Don Norman

this quote to open lectures about form and function for design undergraduates, and I've used it in academic papers, too. Likewise, I can draw from many other quotes, facts, examples, and stories I've noted along the way. So, I can always rely on my collection of notes to prepare a talk or draft an article.

Here's what's interesting: we get good at what we practice, so when you practice noting things down, your mind gets into the habit of noticing interesting stuff. It begins with a growing ability to distinguish between essential and redundant information, but after a while, you start to spot unexpected connections between ideas. A passage in a book reminds you of a scene from a film, or an idea from a lecture close to a song lyric. A noticing mind is like a clever spider weaving a web of ideas.

Before we even put in place a note-taking system we can already identify the benefits of taking notes:

Note-taking benefits

Observational skills: Noting things down trains the mind to become attentive and discerning. Over time, this practice leads to the ability to distinguish between meaningful and irrelevant information.

Enhanced connections: By taking notes, the mind naturally draws connections between concepts. We are pattern-seeking creatures, so this is the natural way our brain works. These links often lead to new ideas or a deeper understanding of existing ones as information converges to form a personal web of knowledge.

Creative thinking: A mind accustomed to associating ideas is prone to creative thinking. In fact, to connect unrelated ideas is almost the definition of creativity.

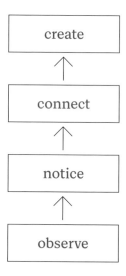

It's hard to gloss over the transformative power of consistent observation and note-taking. A note-taking habit expands the boundaries of our understanding and elevates our creative mindset. A noticing mind can tune in to what's meaningful, like a maestro attuned to perfect pitch.

Mind²

A smart note-taking system is like a support structure for your thinking. It helps pick out good ideas, guides you in navigating a world of overflowing information, and sharpens your point of view. But taking notes is easy; you write down your thoughts and ideas in a notebook. Right?

Wrong. Writing notes in a notebook is as helpful as burying a treasure without drawing the map. Sure, you can capture information quickly in a notebook, but years later, when you want to find that half-remembered quote or that insightful story, how do you know where to find it? On what page of which notebook?

There are productive ways to take notes and unproductive ways to take notes. Most people do the latter.

Gathering information is easy, retrieving it is hard. If you bury notes in notebooks, you can only revisit them when you know what you're looking for and where to find it. A good note-taking system holds my thoughts and reveals them even after I forgot they were there.

A note-taking system is not just a memory aid, it should mirror the natural workings of the brain and *connect* information. Not lineary like a datasheet, organically like a mindmap. The mind is powerful when associating ideas, not when storing them in a list.

A good note-taking system accomplishes three things: it reduces friction and allows you to gather notes quickly; it locates information when you need it; and finally, it stimulates serendipity.*

---

*   *Serendipity is the joy of a happy coincidence or unexpected discovery.*

Functions of a note-taking system

- Gather
- Locate
- Retrieve
- Serendipity

What if you could have a database of the best insights, thoughts, ideas, facts, quotes, and stories you have ever known? All the things you know that sit just beyond your consciousness's reach. What if everything you know could be interconnected, like a personal knowledge web?

Such a database would **double the capacity of your mind**. It would make you more creative, productive, and aware of the world around you. Is this possible? It's not only possible, but it's also remarkably simple, with a note-taking system called *Deep Noting*.

Deep noting

Many months ago, while writing this book, I was taking a shower in the half-awake morning daze every parent knows so well when a thought entered my mind fully formed: *Writing is not magic; it's a process you can follow.* Surrounded by steam, covered in soap, and holding a bottle of shampoo, I said out loud, "Writing is not Magic, it's Design!"

Ironically, the moment felt magical. The insight was entirely beyond my conscious control. Similar anecdotes abound, from scientific breakthroughs: Archimedes discovered how to measure an object's volume while taking a bath, to artistic inspiration: one morning in 1964, Paul McCartney woke up with the complete tune for "Yesterday" in his head.

People often describe sudden breakthroughs as if an idea was planted directly into their heads. The Greeks used to believe the source of knowledge was the Muses, the inspirational goddesses of literature, science, and the arts, who whispered wisdom into the ears of lucky listeners. But scientists now interpret these flashes of insight as aspects of the creative process; they think good ideas depend not on how much information you gather but on the **unique connections** you make between data.

When we learn, our mind does more than expand on what we already know; instead, the mind connects new information with past knowledge stored in long-term memory. For instance, if you already have a solid understanding of mammals, you find it easier to learn about whales because the mind naturally associates related ideas. When learning, we don't pile up facts haphazardly like a clumsy computer;

instead, like a master weaver, the mind is always knitting information together into a tapestry of knowledge.

The mind's knack for associating ideas supports learning and fuels creativity. The brain evolved to make sense of a bewildering array of sensory data; our prehistoric ancestors lived and died in a mysterious world of lightning storms, earthquakes, and wild animals. Early humans had to learn fast and understand how things were related. As a result, we are the fortunate heirs of a mind constantly seeking meaning and patterns between things. The mind can't stop making sense.

The mind fills in gaps when information is incomplete or ambiguous. In other words, our brain creates meaning even when it doesn't exist. So, think of your mind not like an encyclopedia but like a neverending novel. An encyclopedia is a collection of unrelated facts, whereas a novel tells a story. And stories make sense.

Our mind constantly collects and connects information, and like a mad genius, it sees the relationships between all the observations, conversations, books, songs, lectures, TV shows, and every experience we ever had. The software is always running in the background: categorising things, clustering similar ideas together, and connecting unrelated information in new and surprising ways.

And now and then, like a muse whispering wisdom, the mind presents a new idea that appears fully formed in our awareness. Our mind often surprises us with a sudden insight, which is just a new connection between unrelated ideas. When this happens, we feel lucky, blessed, and inspired, but insights are the natural product of how our mind works.

Insights may feel like whispers from the muses, but they are the natural result of our brain's sense-making software. Our minds are programmed to move from collecting data to categorising and connecting related information. But it doesn't stop there. For some reason yet unexplained by science, the mind is eager also to link unrelated things to produce insights.

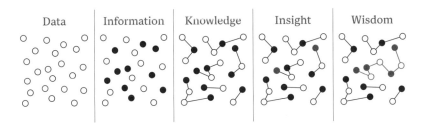

| Data | Information | Knowledge | Insight | Wisdom |

Information vs Knowledge

We live in the Information Age. Information is everywhere, all the time, and freely available to everyone. Unless you consciously try to disconnect, you receive information whether you want to or not. Now that anyone can access the same endless amount of data, are we all equally creative?

The answer is obviously no. Because there is a difference between information and **knowledge**.*

Collecting data helps if you can do something with it. A mind filled with data is about as practical as a messy garage. Sure, you know the information is in your head, but can you find it? And the more you gather, the worse it gets. For data to be valuable, you must tag, sort, and organise it. But collecting and organising is not all: to generate an insight, you have to **connect** ideas. You must transform your mind from a data warehouse to an insight workshop.

*   Data—Wisdom diagram adapted form a diagram designed by David Sommerville.

Insights result from a mind that evolved to associate ideas. This process is beyond our conscious control. But rather than waiting for the muses to bless us, we can leverage the pattern-seeking software evolution left in our brains to trigger new ideas and insights. And we can do it with our notes.

It's been done before, with a technique called *Zettelkasten*.

Zettelkasten

Zettelkasten is a hyper-efficient note-taking tool created by Niklas Luhmann. Luhman (1927–1998) was a German sociologist and an expert in systems theory who used Zettelkasten to write seventy books and hundreds of academic articles during his thirty-year career. Maths is not my strongest point, but I believe that's an average of more than two books a year, on top of all the academic articles.

How did he do this?

Luhmann collected information on index cards. Index cards are small; they can only hold a short handwritten note. This means each card contained a single idea, fact, quote, or any other useful information that Luhmann gathered from his extensive reading. The notes were then stored in an archive (a large piece of wooden furniture with many drawers) and separated by tab dividers. It sounds about as exciting as describing a library, I know. But the system had a twist: the notes were **hypertext**.

These days, hypertext is a common feature of the World Wide Web. Hypertext links pieces of text together; it allows people to navigate information by clicking on links that lead to related content. Now, Luhmann could navigate his physical archive much like we navigate the internet today, albeit much slower. For instance, Luhmann could move from a note about *Socialism* to a note with a related point about *Democracy*. In other words, Luhmann's note-taking system anticipated Wikipedia by fifty years.

With Zettelkasten, the goal is **connection**, not collection. So Luhmann identified each note with a unique ID and connected it to other related notes. This was a painstaking effort but paid off in remarkable productivity for decades.

Fortunately, we don't have to be obsessive workaholics to benefit from the Zettelkasten technique. We now have access to digital tools. Strict followers of the Zettelkasten method are often rigid in using the system. But like most designers, I'm a pragmatic person. If personal computers were around in the 1960s, Luhmann would've used them to organise his archive. Also, Zettelkasten was created for Luhmann's specific needs as a sociologist. The needs of designers are more dynamic. The Design historian Victor Margolin, author of a massive two-volume work on World Design History, uses a personal variation of the Zettelkasten system, too.

Deep Noting is a streamlined version of the Zettelkasten. It builds on the valuable principles of Luhmann's method, but it's a more versatile note-taking system **designed to generate insights**. The goal is not to amass vast quantities of information like a mad librarian but to fuel the creative process and trigger new ideas.

Deep Noting amplifies the natural ability of the human mind to combine ideas while expanding its memory; it's a note-taking system **and** an upgrade for your brain. Let me show you how it works.

The mind is for having ideas, not holding them.

David Allen

What you need

First, you need notecards. Most people use classic ruled index cards, but designers may prefer blank notecards so that they can sketch on them, too. Notecards can be any size as long as they fit in your pocket (I prefer A7). And you need a pen.

I always carry a pack of blank notecards, which I can easily store on my pocketbook agenda. My notecards are a reliable daily companion, and I can sketch or write on them whenever necessary. I make it a habit of reaching for my notecards when I'm waiting for the bus or an appointment.

I write quick notes on my notecards when I'm on the subway, attending a lecture or presentation, listening to a podcast or watching a documentary, and even while talking with friends and they say something clever. When I'm reading, I prefer to scribble notes on the margins or as a comment on a PDF or an e-book. But you can use notecards for that, too.

The purpose of notecards is to capture everything that comes your way without any judgement. Always pay attention when something tickles your curiosity. Gather everything from quotes to song lyrics or a surprising fact you heard during a podcast. Notecards serve as a temporary holder for ideas and release your mind from the burden of remembering everything. Takes notes without a filter: if it's interesting, you note it down; that's the only rule. The point is to **capture** information, not analyse it.

In the deep noting system, these daily notes are called **capture notes**.

Capture notes

Capture notes gather everything that comes your way that draws your attention. You write them quickly without worrying if they're any good or valuable. Capture notes can be divided into two:

1. **Everyday** notes that hold the spontaneous thoughts and ideas that pop into your head as you go about your day;

2. **Content** notes, which are thoughts and ideas you have while consuming media.

Everyday notes

Everyday notes hold the thoughts that come into our minds throughout the day. They often occur unexpectedly, for instance, while showering, walking, or talking to friends. In such moments, our mind tends to wander freely and often lands on an epiphany (a moment of sudden revelation). I'm sure you've experienced working for days on a project without much progress when one day, while walking in a park, a solution hits you. That's an epiphany.

But epiphanies escape our minds like fish slipping through a wide net. So, we must capture them as notes.

If a spontaneous thought pops up, you scribble it on a card. You will regret it if you don't. Don't worry if it's good because you can't tell yet. Your cards will often surprise you later. Capture everything without judgement and separate the wheat from the chaff later.

Content notes

We write content notes when we enjoy media such as books, articles, podcasts, films, songs, or lectures. In these moments, your mind opens to someone else's thoughts, whether a singer, a podcaster, a writer, or a teacher. Reading a book is a classic example. A sentence can suddenly arrest you like lightning in a clear sky, even while reading distractedly. Your whole day seems to pivot at that moment. Enchanted by the sudden insight, you underline the passage and quickly scribble something on the margin.

Develop the habit of noticing what stands out. Consume content and capture everything that sparks your interest. It could be a quote, an unexpected fact, an insight, or a story that moves you. Now, when reading, we often underline or highlight a passage. When listening, we make mental notes. Unfortunately, both mental notes and highlighting are useless in isolation.

So here's a **key rule** of note taking:

If you underline a passage, you **must** write why it's important. Write on the margins if you're reading a book or annotate a PDF when reading on a screen, but write it down. Otherwise, you'll forget why it matters. But more importantly, if the passage you're underlining reminds you of something else, perhaps another idea or even another note you took, **always write it down**. Even if it seems unrelated or silly. Write it down **especially** if it seems unrelated or silly. Insights often arrive from strange and unexpected connections.

As you develop the habit of capturing notes, your mind attunes to interesting stuff, like a musician developing an ear for melody. Sometimes, three hours of a podcast discussion may suddenly light up with a clever insight, and with habit, your mind will alert you to these moments. Taking notes is transformative. The act of note-taking fine-tunes our awareness of the world around us.

Capture notes rules

Capture notes are always judgement free, the point is to **capture everything** that stands out. Now, notes can accumulate and become a mess, to avoid this you must follow these rules:

1. **Notes are atomic**: one idea per notecard. Each note must be a single indivisible idea (like an atom) and no longer than a short paragraph.

2. **Notes are brief**: notecards are small for a reason. Get into the habit of identifying the essential. Keep your notes short. One paragraph is ideal. If a note is two paragraphs long, break it into two notes, or summarise it into one.

3. **Notes with references**: always write down where the idea, fact, quote, story or whatever else, came from.

4. **Notes are connected**: if your observation reminds you of another idea always write it down; it could be something as simple as "this reminds of x."

The Review

The next step is the weekly review. At the end of a week, you have a stack of everyday notes gathered from daily life and content notes from the media you consume. Now, you must sit down and process them.

During the review, you sort between notes to keep and to discard. At this stage, many notes are discarded. Remember that brilliant idea you had while showering? Turns out it's nonsense. The insightful quote you captured from a book? Dull. And so you move through your notecards one by one until you find something worth keeping.

If a note is worth keeping, you turn it into a **deep note**.

Deep Notes

How do you write a deep note?

You start by **reviewing** capture notes. We have seen how capture notes gather (1) everyday fleeting thoughts and (2) ideas collected while consuming content. Capture notes fuel the deep noting system, but the system's goal is to produce Deep Notes.

Deep notes are the notes you store to use later. They make up an **archive of interconnected ideas** that make sense of the things you study, the research you conduct, and the topics that interest you.

The archive is made of two elements: plaintext files and a folder. There is no need for an expensive and complex piece of software that takes time to master and requires endless fiddling with options, features, or tools. If you prefer fancy software, that's fine too; whatever works. But I urge you to give the plaintext system at least a try.

Deep noting

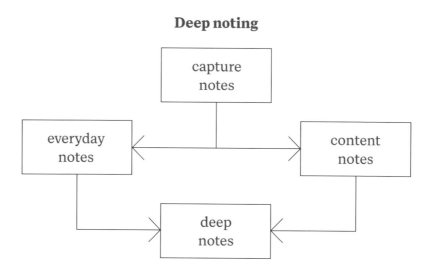

Plaintext

To turn a capture note into a deep note, you create a digital version of it. A deep note holds only one idea, so a deep note is a single digital file. My preferred file format for deep notes is *plaintext*, which means using the all powerful TXT file.

Why TXT files? Unlike proprietary formats like DOC, TXT files are not owned by any specific company, which prevents them from being locked down by a large corporation such as Microsoft. Plaintext ensures that your content remains yours.

Plaintext files are small, simple, searchable by any operating system, easy to edit, and to back up. You don't have to worry about text formatting, which saves time while writing. All you need to work with plaintext is a simple text editor.

A text editor is any computer program that opens, creates, and edits plaintext files. Text editors come installed on most operating systems, like Windows (Notepad) and Mac (TextEdit). A text editor is not a word processor. Word processors are designed to produce polished final documents, whereas text editors focus on character representation.

You may be wondering why use plaintext over Microsoft Word or a sophisticated note-taking software like Evernote. Here's a summary of plaintext advantages:

Plaintext advantages

- **Future proof**: plaintext files do not require specific software to open or edit. They work on any computer regardless of operating system. You can open, edit, and print a TXT file as long as there are computers. This is crucial because your notes should not be written for a specific project but for life.
- **Independence**: TXT files are software independent, which means you will never be subjected to a company updating their software or increasing their subscription rates. Also, if you change your mind, you can import TXT files to any software you prefer.
- **Lightness**: TXT files are perhaps the lightest file type. Any operating system can search keywords in a large archive of plaintext files and offer results in seconds, and a complete backup takes seconds as well.
- **Robust**: I have never seen a corrupted TXT file. The information it stores is so simple it's pretty much incorruptible. Robustness also contributes to making your archive future proof.

In short, plaintext files are lightweight, future-proof, quick, independent, effective, robust, and reliable. They don't require sophisticated software because the humble Notepad (Windows) or TextEdit (Mac) will do. Also, plaintext does not distract you with formatting, layout, font choice, colours, or other options. Plaintext files hold your notes so that you may focus on your ideas.

If plaintext files are simple, the archive is even simpler. It's a folder.

One Folder

Deep notes are stored in a single folder. The only thing a complex hierarchy of subfolders achieves is that you don't remember where your information is years later (sometimes *weeks* later). If you open your [Deep Notes] folder, you know all your notes are there. Even if you have thousands of notes, the note you're looking for is there. And since your notes are plaintext, you can quickly search for keywords and find what you're looking for within seconds.

The organisation of your notes is neither hierarchical nor based on categories. It's not hierarchical because no overarching notes include other sub-notes; each note is atomic, meaning a single idea clearly expressed in your words. Deep notes are linked with other deep notes to form a network, and each note is as important as any other note. This system of linked notes allows for threads of thought to emerge organically, one idea leading to another, that leads to another and another, and so on.

Deep noting is valuable in the unique streams of thought that emerge from connecting ideas, not in the accumulation of unrelated notes.

For the same reasons, the system is not based on categories. Each note contains a single idea connected to other ideas: facts, quotes, stories, or even your ideas and thoughts, each referencing where it came from and a comment in your own words. But the crucial point is not to store these notes into categories; for instance, you could create sub-folders named [facts] or [quotes], but the point is not to gather specific information but to connect each idea into the whole of your thinking. The point is to make sense of information and generate insights, not to develop a personal encyclopedia.

Deep noting process

Here's an illustration of the deep noting process.

Years ago, during the coffee break of an academic design conference, I was waiting for a refill of the typically watery and tasteless coffee you get at such events when, amid the noise of multiple conversations, I overheard the phrase 'beautifully useful'.

I don't recall the context of the conversation at all, and I couldn't identify who said it. But I remember the phrase hitting me like a burst of sunlight through heavy clouds. I snatched my notecards and scribbled something down just as I got my coffee refill. Not giving it another thought, I continued with my day.

By the end of the week, I was reviewing my notes when I came across a notecard that read:

Design beautifully useful things...
form follows function?

I had half-forgotten about this note, so it felt like finding a treasure. The idea resonated, so I turned it into a deep note. What followed was simple:

1. Open the text editor
2. Write the note
3. Write the reference

First, I wrote down the essential information. In this case, the note was something I overheard, so there was no reference to an article, a book, or any other form of media.

The next step is crucial. I must explain why the note is **meaningful**. As it stands, the note is hazy and unclear. Why does it matter? Why did it move me? I had to reflect to articulate the meaning lurking beneath the surface. Writing a deep note requires intense focus; you can't rush it or write while distracted by other tasks.

After a few failed attempts I settled on the paragraph:

Design is the craft of creating beautifully useful things. It's not art, where beauty is the goal, nor is it engineering, concerned only with functionality. It combines art and technology, transcending both as a unique discipline: Design.

The paragraph deepened the phrase 'beautifully useful,' making it personally significant. This example illustrates how **writing is thinking**. Compare my initial annotation, *"design beautifully useful things... form follows function?"* to the clarified idea above. Writing deep notes extracts meaning from hazy ideas, like squeezing juice from an orange.

Nietzsche famously said that *"our writing tools are also working on our thoughts,"* the German philosopher was referring to his typewriter. Still, we can expand on what he meant to include writing methods and techniques. Writing deep notes forces you to reflect and helps you to think in an interconnected way.

A deep note on its own is already valuable. It's an idea richly distilled like whiskey, a thought pared down to its essence. But when you combine a deep note with another deep note, it becomes larger than the sum of its parts. Like John Lennon and Paul McCartney being more brilliant together than alone.

Deep notes must be **connected to other deep notes** and plugged into your growing web of thought.

Connect

When gathering information with capture notes, be mindful of any connections that pop into your head and note them down, too. This way, when writing a deep note, you already have a hint of the notes it can connect with.

Even though I have over 2,000 deep notes in my archive, I can remember the notes I want to link. And on the rare occasions I don't remember, a search with a few keywords quickly reveals what I'm looking for.

In the example above, I noted, *"form follows function?"* That short annotation was a reminder of where the phrase 'beautifully useful' could fit. So, during the review, I knew I wanted to link the note *beautifully useful* to a deep note in my archive called *form follows function*.

To connect deep notes, write the filename of the note you want to connect with at the bottom. If you want to connect more notes, add more filenames. That's it.

I wrote *form follows function* at the bottom of my deep note which now looked like this:

Design is the craft of creating beautifully useful things. It's not art, where beauty is the goal, nor is it engineering, concerned only with functionality. It combines art and technology, transcending both as a unique discipline: Design.

Link: *form follows function.*

And then an extraordinary thing happened.

Serendipity

When I reviewed my *form follows function* note I noticed it was linked with a note called *known to be useful*, which read as follows:

Have nothing in your house that you do not know to be useful, or believe to be beautiful. William Morris

I had forgotten about this quote, so stumbling upon it was a pleasant surprise. But what intrigued me further was the way the notes resonated with each other. It was as if their meaning was enriched when reading them side-by-side. Like combining a touch of blue with a snip of yellow to create a richer shade of green.

When you archive a deep note, you're not passively storing away an isolated piece of wisdom. A deep note is not archived but **plugged into** a stream of thought; a deep note flows like a tributary stream into a larger river. I could follow that stream, with each idea flowing into the next. I could now follow that stream with each idea flowing into the next.

The reward of the deep noting system doesn't lay in accumulating knowledge but in the gradual creation of personal threads of thought woven from the most compelling ideas you've ever thought or encountered. Following these threads often leads to **flashes of insight**, **serendipity** when unrelated ideas are happily combined, and **sharper thinking** because each note is written carefully as a single atomic idea, a thought pared to its essence.

The direct links between deep notes are the heart of the deep noting system. But there is another level of connection— the cluster.

Clustering

The *beautifully useful* deep note fits my ongoing interest in design and form theory. Naturally, my deep notes folder already had some notes about these topics.

As we've seen before, creating subfolders becomes unmanageable, unruly, and inefficient. But it is helpful to group deep notes into general topics like Design Theory. No problem. Here's another way plaintext files come in handy: you can #tag them.

To cluster by topic, add #hashtags to your notes. These hashtags should be broad categories, for example, #design-thinking, #cognition, or #writing. For the *beautifully useful* note, I added #design-theory and #form. There's no limit to the tags you can add to a deep note.

The purpose of the tags is to cluster notes into a constellation of ideas. In this case, ideas on Design Theory and Form. Here's how the finalised deep note looks:

Filename: *beautifully useful*

#design-theory #form

Design is the craft of creating beautifully useful things. It's not art, where beauty is the goal, nor is it engineering, concerned only with functionality. It combines art and technology, transcending both as a unique discipline: Design.

Link: form follows function

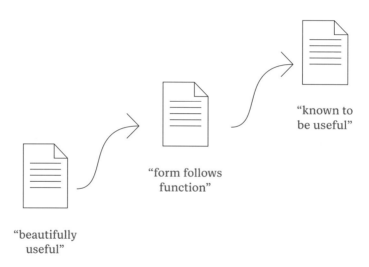

"beautifully useful"

"form follows function"

"known to be useful"

FileNaming

Deep notes should have a descriptive file name. The deep note in our example is called *beautifully useful*. Here are other examples from my deep noting archive:

100 untalented persons (a note on a research study from the 1980s that showed 100 untalented persons don't match the output of a single talented individual);

an open mind is not an empty head (a quote from Edward Tufte about the pitfals of being uninformed);

framing (a note on how designers use frames when working to temporarily establish order to the often messy design problems).

The file name and the hashtags have enough information to locate your notes when you need them quickly; retrieval, after all, is more important than gathering and archiving.

Retrieval

It's a good idea to keep a list of all the hashtags you create so you know what you can look for later. I keep a special note called "0_tags" in my deep noting folder for that purpose. The "zero" ensures the 0_tags file is the top file in the deep notes folder. When I create a new tag, I add it to my 0_tags note.

Let's look at another example on how hashtags and links promote retrieval and trigger serendipity.

Say, I'm writing a piece on *design thinking.* Here's my process on day one: I search the folder for #design-thinking and identify 70 notes. I create a PDF with the 70 notes on design thinking and print them. If you prefer not to print, you can copy and paste your notes into a blank document and work from there. But I think there are advantages to holding your notes and physically rearranging and reviewing them.

I hold my design thinking notes and read them with full attention. Some are already interlinked. But here's what's interesting: some design thinking notes are linked to notes with tags such as #creativity or #innovation. So I can return to my computer and print those, too.

#design-thinking

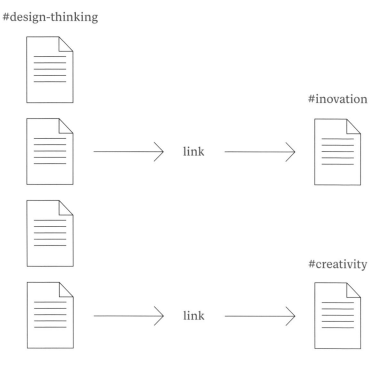

#inovation

link

#creativity

link

You see, the deep noting system reveals the notes you need exactly when you need them. And some connections will surprise you. The deep noting system saves you the impossible effort of holding all this interconnected information in your head. So, your mind is free to have ideas because you created a **duplicate of your brain** using a simple folder and plaintext files.

On day one of writing my article on Design Thinking, I already have notes neatly clustered into topics. And the notes are already organised into a chain of interrelated thoughts. I only had to think about the links between the notes **once**; having done that prior work, I can sit down and write.

Atomic notes

Deep notes are **atomic**. Regardless of its topic, each note holds a single idea that stands by itself. For notes to be useful for multiple projects, they must be single and independent.

For instance, most people organise their notes about a book they've read in a single document that contains all their highlights, quotes, and thoughts. This is an example of how tools can limit how we think. If you paste your notes into a giant document with multiple pages of facts, quotes, examples, and so on, then how do you think?

You think linearly. From top to bottom. Your notes are *forced* into a linear structure, so you think in a sequence of A, then B, then C.

Linear thinking

$$A \longrightarrow B \longrightarrow C \longrightarrow \ldots$$

Now, if instead you write atomic notes, and each idea stands on its own, what happens? You get a constellation of ideas. You're no longer thinking linearly but organically. Note A may lead to B or be linked to Z, Y, or J. Your ideas develop as a living web of multiple threads of thought.

Constellation of ideas

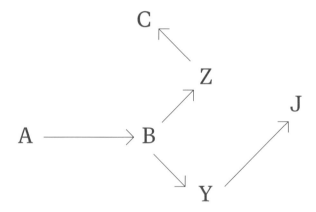

Writing modularity applies at every level. Deep notes are the smallest module of the NODE writing method because you can rearrange and reuse them. And the more deep notes you write, the richer your archive gets because you're elaborating lines of reasoning and trains of thought.

We want one idea per note because deep notes are building blocks. When playing with Legos, you can rearrange the blocks into any shape; it's the same with your notes, but instead of castles or police stations, you're connecting notes to form deeper ideas.

Navigate your mind

The deep noting system allows you to navigate the landscape of your mind. Your mind is an intricate web of thoughts, memories, facts, dreams, fears, ideas, and so on. This web is shapcd like a personal landscape containing everything that matters to you. It's also rich with undiscovered connections and insights. Of course, the problem is finding the insights you need when you need them. After all, your mind is not filled only with the good bits.

If your head is anything like mine, then it's a mess. It is an entangled, foggy, and often scary place that holds my fears, hopes, ambitions, and quirks, all running to the soundtrack of cartoon theme songs from the 1980s I can't seem to forget, regardless of how hard I try. On top of that, there's the heavy layer of everyday troubles, schedules, duties, meetings, and all the boring bits of adult life. Why would I want to navigate **that**?

But what if you could turn inward and explore only the insightful and brilliant bits of your thinking? What if there was a way to explore your mind for treasure, meaning, insights, unique connections, and personal observations?

That's what the Deep Noting system does. It offers a map to a second brain holding only the insightful bits. And you can visit it whenever you need inspiration, information, and wisdom.

Make haste slowly

Creating deep notes is a deliberatly slow process. Linking the notes is demanding because you have to search for each connection inside your folder. But remember that deep noting is based on the Zettelkasten method, which was much harder to navigate.* With Zettelkasten, Luhmann could't search his archive using CTRL+F, he opened heavy wooden drawers and flickered through cardboard tabs.

Full disclosure: some software can automatically link your notes by creating direct wikilinks between plaintext files. But the danger of software such as Notion or Obsidian (for instance) is that we tend to get carried away with all the features and maintain the archive instead of focusing on developing ideas. Nevertheless, if you have the mental fortitude not to be swept away into the distracting aspects of entertaining software, then, by all means, use it.

If you're like me (easily distracted), I think there is something to be gained in the natural friction of the deep noting system. It forces you to slow down and concentrate. The system demands that you reflect on what you gathered instead of collecting more information. In the age of high-speed connectivity and information overflow, slowing down is rare. But slowing down and concentrating are two elements you can't dismiss if you aim to produce creative work that adds value.

Meaningful progress takes time and effort, but slow progress adds up. Imagine spending one hour daily practising a complicated scale on the piano. It doesn't look like you're making much progress on any given weekday, but after a month of practice, you eventually master it. All research on performance shows that slow progress is more effective than occasional periods of strenuous work. The mind needs time to recover from deep focus, but it pays off in the long run.

---

*   *And yet, some authors (such as New York Times best-selling non-fiction author Ryan Holiday) still use zettelkasten in its analog version, and swear by it.*

Same with note-taking. If you make a daily effort of writing notes on your fleeting thoughts and the media you consume, and you spend 30-minutes or so every week reviewing them and creating deep notes, it adds up. Imagine that, from now on, you write as little as two notes everyday for a whole year. That's 730 capture notes. Now, let's assume less than half of those are actually good and turn into deep notes. In one year you'll have an invaluable collection of 300 interconnected deep notes about a variety of topics. You didn't produce much on a daily scale, but you made a huge leap in one year.

Every deep note you write adds up, and you can see it, which creates what psychologists call a *positive feedback loop*. Deep noting is an investment. As time passes and you keep adding notes to your archive, the thinking threads grow, the connections become richer, and the potential for new insights increases.

Deep Noting Workflow

The deep noting workflow follows these steps:

Noticing: Capture all the ideas that resonate from your everyday life and the media you experience.

Reviewing: Form the habit of processing your capture notes at the end of the week; sort out what stays and what gets discarded. If a note resonates, turn it into a deep note.

Archiving: Create a digital archive of simple plaintext files and a folder for deep notes.

Capture notes feed the deep noting system, but the goal of the system is to generate deep notes; to create a deep note follow these steps:

1. Review your weekly capture notes
2. Write down the notes you want to keep in a plaintext file
3. Reference where you gathered the information from
4. Sensemaking: explain, in your own words, why the note is meaningful
5. Connecting: link the deep note with other deep notes
6. Clustering: #tag the deep note with broad categories (like #design-thinking)

Now that you know how to capture notes, process them, and create deep notes. Deep notes should always follow these principles:

Deep Noting Principles

- Atomicity: write a single idea per note;
- Connection: notes must be linked to other notes;
- Discoverability: #tag your notes, so they're easy to locate;
- Personal: always use your own words, even when explaining the ideas of others;
- References: write **notes with references**, not references with notes
- Notes for life: Notes are not just useful for a single project but for a lifetime. Even if you don't use your notes for a current project, you prepare material for future efforts

The rationale behind these principles is simple, but the result is astonishing: you will **double** the cognitive power of your mind because the Deep Noting system functions like an external brain. When you upload files to an external hard drive disk, your computer runs faster, right? The processor is lighter and can assign resources to *process* information instead of spending them to *store* information.

Deep Noting works like a backup disk; it frees your mind to think. But while a backup disk stores information, Deep Noting stores **and** connects information. Deep Noting is a cognitive superpower

You can build
a strong, sound,
and artful
structure.
You can build a
structure in
such a way that
it causes people
to want to keep
turning pages.

John McPhee

Outline

You collected information and written deep notes, and you feel prepared to shape that material into writing. Transforming a collection of deep notes into a linear text can be puzzling. Remember, your deep notes mirror how your mind works, which means they're associative and organic. But a text is, inevitably, **linear**. Regardless of how brilliant and interconnected your ideas may be, the text follows a strict sequence of beginning, middle, and end.

Sure, your ideas are naturally connected, but in what order should you present them to your readers? What is the most effective way to communicate the material you gathered as notes?

To preserve the interconnected structure of your deep notes, you can **design an outline**.

The outline is the often neglected part of writing. It's not the idyllic stage of sitting down and letting ideas flow from the pen, nor the exciting note-taking stage when discovering new ideas and engaging with compelling material. And yet, an outline could be the difference between seeing a project through or giving up. Writing without an outline is like setting sail without a chart; you end up wherever the winds blow.

An outline is **a structure that organises the ideas, details, and overall form of a piece of writing**. It serves as a roadmap for the writer, helping to shape ideas into a coherent piece. Outlines can take different forms depending on the nature of the material itself; still, an outline usually includes the key points and the order in which they will be presented.

The typical outline you'll find in most articles, essays, blog posts, or even chapters in a dissertation is the classic essay structure, which goes like this:

1. **Introduction:**
   Opening hook or attention-grabber
   Thesis statement or main idea

2. **Body Paragraphs: Each paragraph structured as:**
   Opening sentence with main idea of the paragraph
   Supporting details or evidence
   Transition sentence to next paragraph

3. **Conclusion:**
   Summary of main points
   Restatement of main idea
   Concluding thoughts (or transition to next section)

There's nothing wrong with this template. The classic essay structure fits almost any occasion, like wearing a black t-shirt and jeans. If you're near a deadline and need to get a writing assignment out of the way, this template offers a clear and solid structure to see you through.

Unfortunately, it's also dull, didactic, and uninspiring. Imagine a graphic designer who designed exclusively in black and white and used only the *Times New Roman* typeface. Sure, you can do a decent job with those elements, but it's probably inappropriate for every project. In other words, the classic essay structure is fine, but it's not the best we can do.

You're writing because you have something to say, you're passionate about a topic, or there's essential information you want to share with others. So make your reader's life easier by designing a structure that fits your ideas.

But how can you shape a constellation of deep notes into a linear text without destroying its web-like form? After all, every text follows a linear sequence: the reader moves from one line to the next, finishing a sentence before starting the next. But while the sequence of sentences may be linear, the inner structure of a text, its overall design, is not.

For example, imagine a long-read news story about a political scandal. The journalist can start with a matter-of-fact narration of how the events unfolded only to shift into a flashback of decades ago: readers then witness how a shady deal sowed the seeds of the present-day political turmoil. When the journalist brings the readers back into the main narrative, they understand how past and present events are connected.

A text must follow a linear sequence, but the ideas can move around a central topic, like planets orbiting the sun. A skilful structure doesn't force ideas into an ill-fitting shape; instead, a clever outline design adds depth, fits your ideas better, and keeps the reader engaged.

The trick is to think non-linearly for as long as possible. Notes are associative, like our thinking patterns, so let's hold on to that mindset for a while. To do this, you must **see** the structure of your text.

So don't write an outline, design it.

How to design an Outline

Let's consider, for example, we had to prepare a lecture for an undergraduate class on *affordances*, an idea popularised by Don Norman in his book "The Design of Everyday Things."

Affordances are perceived relationships between objects and users. They suggest how an object can be used or what actions are possible. Imagine you're facing a door, and you want to open it. An "affordance" is a clue or a hint that the door gives you about how to use it: A flat metal surface implies you should *push*, while a handle or a bar means you should *pull*.

Affordances are important for design. They allow objects to "speak" with their users, hinting at how to use them. There's our **communication problem**. We have to write the lecture notes so that the students can grasp the concept of affordance, internalise it, start noticing it in their everyday lives, and become aware of the idea when designing

The investment in deep noting pays off. I have been interested in affordances for a while, so I've read several books and articles and discussed the topic with my colleagues. So, I have captured information on affordances and written them as deep notes. So, to start writing, we follow these three simple steps:

1. Open the deep notes folder
2. Search for #affordance
3. Print all the notes tagged #affordance

Now, we have a ton of material to work with. Print each note on a separate sheet of paper. Next, spread all the notes on a large table to see every note. If you don't have a big enough table, spread them on the floor or pin them to a board.

The material we face is a personally curated collection of notes on affordances. Next, we must figure out how these notes fit together. The first step is *clustering* them into groups.

Clustering

Remember how your deep notes link with other deep notes? This comes in handy, too, because now you follow a thinking thread of notes like Hansel and Gretel following bread-crumbs. Each note leading to another. At this stage, you may have to print more notes because deep notes on #affordance may lead, for instance, to notes on #usability or #innovation, which wouldn't show up when you first searched your folder.

These thinking threads form natural arguments or ideas we want to explore. So, we cluster them and the notes start to group around different topics.

Interesting ideas emerge, because we see the big picture of how the notes combine into a coherent narrative. This is exciting because it's out of our control. The notes lead the process. Outlining feels more like exploring a territory than imposing order; we're not shaping material but discovering a pattern.

Now, we have a few clusters of deep notes. It's too soon to decide where a particular group will fit in the final piece; for now, give each cluster a name. Let's say you end up with five groups, each one holding a few notes:

- Affordance
- Usability
- Interaction
- Function
- Examples

These five clusters have no particular sequence. They are Lego blocks we can play with without knowing what structure we will build. As we've seen before, the writing process is modular. A module can fit anywhere, depending on what we're building.

The advantage of the modular approach is that it frees you from figuring out in advance what's important, what comes first, or how to end. Don't lock yourself in, nor settle on a structure too soon. It's time to explore. And how do designers explore best? They sketch.

Sketch an outline

Grab your favourite pen or pencil, a sketchbook, a piece of paper or multiple small ones, a tablet, or whatever works. The goal is to experiment with different structures for your clusters. At this stage, you may be tempted to follow a linear structure; try to resist the linear mould and sketch your outline like a *diagram*.

Designers are used to diagrams. A diagram is an illustration that communicates an idea with visuals. Typical examples include the *flowchart* which represents the different steps in a workflow; *venn diagram* which uses overlapping circles to reveal what's common between different groups; or the almighty *mindmap*, which is a visual representation of a web of concepts often used to generate ideas.

A quick diagram sketch is a powerful way to think through a complex idea. Diagrams can reveal patterns and relationships that would be impossible to discover using only words. Here, the designer has an advantage over other writers: designers are visual thinkers by default.

So, it's time to capitalise on your visual thinking skills. You can use diagram sketches to design the outline of any text. Sketch the outline, don't merely pile notes, that's linear thinking. You want to think in networks of interrelated ideas. You have identified how your notes can be clustered into groups. Now, you design an outline structure that holds your ideas together.

Explore different outline shapes. Experiment with structures that emphasise the relationships between the ideas. When you design an outline, you're shaping the material into a coherent form; you order the notes by following your understanding of the material.

Don't worry, you won't have to reinvent the wheel. Writers have been using a powerful narrative structure since the dawn of language: it's called *storytelling*.

Storytelling

Every text tells a story, even nonfiction.

The classic essay structure we find in most texts breaks the unique links between notes and forces ideas into an ill-fitting shape, like a person in a tight sweater.

Don't force your deep notes into an essay structure; tell a story instead. People love stories. Stories are the default format to convey values, morals, ideas, history, or culture. Stories don't bore readers; stories delight them.

Different narrative structures shape stories. Shaping a nonfiction idea as a narrative is fun and enhances your material. A narrative structure makes your writing, your *story*, come alive. Your ideas may be brilliant, but you must find a way to tell a compelling story to your readers. As all comedians know, it's how you tell a joke that matters.

And yes, you can follow these principles for academic writing as well. In fact, you should. Helen Sword is a researcher concerned with the quality of academic writing, and she is convinced that academics should tell stories, not bore their readers with unreadable prose lacking spark or individuality. We return to the problem of communication. What good is there in an academic paper or an unreadable dissertation? Your research is only useful if you communicate its findings.

Academics who write successful books (books that people actually read) are storytellers. Nobel prize winner Richard Feynman's books are a joy to read, even if you know nothing about Physics (I definitely don't). Feynman captures your attention because he tells a story.

A story is a powerful communication format. If you want to control a room filled with unruly toddlers, try shouting, *"Let me tell you a story..."* they will immediately stop and gather around eagerly waiting for you to begin. Adults are the same. If you don't believe me, check the subscription figures of streaming companies. People love stories so much they stay up late on a weekday, binging them.

Does this mean you must start your nonfiction with "Once upon a time"? No, in fact, most stories don't. We can use **narrative structures** to outline our texts without adopting a storytelling writing style.

What's your story?

What's the story behind our *affordance* example? After printing our deep notes and spreading them on a table or pinning them to a wall, we clustered them into five groups: affordance, usability, interaction, function, and examples.

There are many ways you can use those topics to tell a story. It depends on the material. Imagine you gather many exciting examples of everyday objects and their affordances. We can structure the story with a central thread covering the concepts while a meandering line of examples moves in and out of the central narrative:

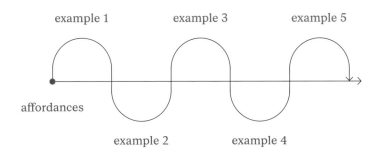

In this outline, we explain the ideas associated with *affordances* following a linear logic but interspersed with tangents where we illustrate our points with real-life examples.

Here's another way we could tackle it. Imagine one of the examples that stands out; let's say we can explain all the ideas of affordances by exploring the example of a washing machine control panel. So, we invert our structure.

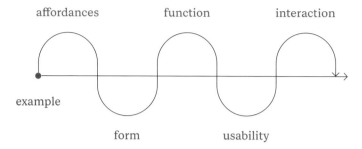

The linear timeline is now the story of that case study, and the tangents are more abstract ideas about affordances. This approach would be good because it moves from the particular to the general. It gives readers concrete experiences they can relate to and build on to explain more abstract ideas about design.

There's no ideal recipe here. The structure of a text emerges from the connections you made in your deep notes. Deep note connections flow from note to note to form a geometry of patterns, shapes, and structures. In other words, each outline is based on a specific set of notes, so each outline has a unique structural design.

It's important to give yourself the time and space to work with your notes to discover the best outline design that fits your material and tells a story. You may settle on an outline design and move on to drafting, only to find it doesn't work, and you have to adapt or redesign the outline. That's fine; it happens all the time. Writing, like design, is an iterative process.

The outline GPS

Settle on an outline that fits the material, makes your story come alive, and communicates effectively.

Pin your outline on the wall before your desk so you see it as you write. This is now your gps. When writing, the outline orients you like the north-star guiding a sailor. As you write, you can move back and forth between your notes and your outline design to check if you're on the right track

Drafting is about shaping your material into a form guided by your outline. You should always have your outline at hand to orient you. The outline tells you where you are and where your writing needs to go, like a global navigation system (GPS) while driving.

During the drafting stage, I like to print the outline and hang it on the wall in my office, right in front of me, so I can raise my eyes from the keyboard and check where I'm at. It's a helpful way never to lose track of the big picture, how the pieces work together, how one idea leads to another, and so on. This way, you can concentrate on details and particular parts without losing the overall idea.

Equipped with your outline design and a stack of deep notes, you can start drafting your text.

In short

The outline workflow:
1. Print all the deep notes you have on a topic
2. Spread them on a surface or pin them to a wall
3. Cluster the notes into groups by following their links
4. Sketch outlines as narrative structures
5. Chose an outline design

Write drunk; edit sober.

Attributed to Ernest Hemingway

Draft

Once you have enough material and an outline, it's time to draft your text. A draft is a first attempt at a finished piece of writing; its role is remarkably similar to a rough prototype during a design project. A draft, like a prototype, is there to be tested. It's a way to check if the ideas flow, if anything is missing, if it works, if other people understand it, and if they don't, what parts need clarification.

In short, with a draft, you can have **feedback** from yourself and from others. You can read it and check if it works. You can give it to a colleague, a friend, or a spouse and ask for tips on improving it. If you're pursuing a master's or PhD degree, a draft is what you send your supervisor for advice.

By the way, did you notice you obliterated blank page anxiety? Whether you're writing a chapter for a dissertation, a first draft for a post, or a newsletter, the process remains the same: all you need to do is copy and paste the material (your deep notes) into a blank page. That's it; there's your rough first draft. It needs work, of course, but it gives you something to work with, instead of a blank page to stare at.

Drafting can be challenging because your deep notes are the product of intense concentration and are well-worded paragraphs; often, when you try to expand on a deep note, it falls short. The writing comes out clunky and clumsy, which leads to frustration and the infamous *writer's block*. That's the reason why there is a golden rule which accomplished writers almost universally accept:

The Golden Rule of Writing

Always separate the *drafting* and *editing* stages of writing. This is important for short pieces and imperative for long ones. Never edit as you draft. Get the words down on paper fast and edit them later, slowly.

How to draft

Drafting is based on your outline and deep notes. The outline works as the roadmap, or GPS, so keep it nearby when you're drafting. For the deep notes, you can roughly copy and paste them into a blank document in the order suggested by your outline.

Deep Notes contain distilled ideas, like a compressed file you must unpack. Deep notes are written like slightly longer aphorisms. So when drafting, you'll need to **elaborate** on your ideas, and any **connections** between ideas must be clarified for the reader's benefit.

Consider readers like designers consider the *users* of their designs. For a designer, the user is front and centre of his concerns. A design *has to work*; it must function correctly. And a design must be clear in how it works. A design shouldn't frustrate the user. You don't want a person staring at a coffee machine you designed and wondering how to operate it, do you?

Of course not. It's the same with writing. You may think you collected a bunch of clever, insightful, and wonderful ideas in your notes, and it all makes perfect sense together. We must always return to the problem of communication of writing. You want to convey your message to your reader with as little friction as possible. So *readability* stands for writing, like *usability* stands for design.

A high level of readability is based on clarity and precision. Your writing should always aim for clarity and be as precise as possible. A goal of good writing is for the text to be so clear that the reader doesn't have to go back and reread it. Do not frustrate the reader. Instead, grab your reader's hand and guide her along your text as if you're taking a good friend for a walk while telling a story. How can you do this?

The draft stage contains two basic tasks
1. Elaborate
2. Linking

Elaborate

Elaborate on the ideas contained in deep notes. Drafting requires elaboration. And elaboration involves extending your ideas: when you elaborate on a point, you add details, examples, analogies or explanations, which enhance the information you're presenting. It's a way of clarifying and deepening your ideas. You can think of elaboration as adding more details and stretching your thoughts, like a musician expanding on a musical line.

Elaboration bridges the gap between your thoughts and the reader's understanding. We elaborate because we care about getting our message across. More information and supporting details clarify our views, especially when the text deals with abstract ideas. When elaborating, you should define vague concepts or offer examples that clarify them.

Without elaboration, writing may be vague and difficult to understand. Expanding on your ideas and providing additional context ensures the message is communicated and readers can engage with your ideas.

Linking

Linking involves clarifying the connections between the points in your writing. It requires additional writing to show how one idea relates to another. Think of it as creating bridges between your thoughts. Just as a well-linked chain forms a strong whole, effective linking in writing strengthens the coherence of your text, making it easier for readers to follow your ideas.

Both elaboration and linking require, well, more writing. This can be intimidating because while your deep notes are personal annotations you wrote for yourself, a draft is supposed to be read by someone else. Or at least, it's the first version of a text another person will read. And so the dreadful inner critic emerges to stop you from advancing. You mustn't let the inner critic win.

The weapons of the inner critic are imposture syndrome, procrastination, and undue criticism. Ignore him. Remember, getting the first draft out of the way is the first step towards writing a good one.

Recover the golden rule of writing *write drunk, edit sober*. In other words, your first draft should be rough. My PhD supervisor used to tell me to send him a "crappy first draft." Only a novice expects a first draft to be anything but rough and unpolished. Experienced writers know first drafts are poor, so they write them as quickly as possible. The important thing is to have something to work with: writing is rewriting. Here are some techniques to overcome the inner critic.

Generative writing

Writers often describe their writing process as refinement and elimination, like sculpting. For instance, Stephen Fry, a British author, said that you wouldn't start a sculpture by taking a bit of clay and shaping it into a perfect nose, and then take another bit of clay and do a toe, and then a bit of hair. Instead, you place a block of clay on your table and slowly shape it into a human form. And then, when you do get to the nose, you refine it, add detail, and perfect it.

It's the same with writing. You must have the whole mass of writing in front of you so you can work. Write down as much as possible to shape it into a statue later. This means writing without concern for spelling, grammatical correctness, if you repeat words, or anything like that. Generating words is all that matters at this stage. Aim for quantity, not quality.

With generative writing, you plug into your stream of conscience and write down the words as they come. No criticism, no judging, no second guessing. Just writing.

This is all good, but when you're facing a stubborn draft that won't progress, what should we do? Easy: get up and walk.

Only thoughts that come by walking have any value.

Friedrich Nietzsche

Take your ideas for a walk

One of my favourite tools when I'm stuck with a draft is to go for a walk with an audio recorder. Nowadays, a mobile phone will do, but you risk being interrupted by a call. You should pick a familiar spot so you're not distracted by someplace new, but the place should be interesting. I prefer a park or a garden, but a nice neighbourhood with narrow streets also does the trick for me.

You go for a stroll and keep your current draft in your awareness as you walk. This is not easy at first, especially if you're not used to it. Cal Newport, a nonfiction author and computer scientist from Georgetown University, calls it *productive meditation*.

The key to productive meditation is to focus on the issue at hand, allowing your mind to explore different angles and potential solutions. To maximise this effort, you should speak your thoughts aloud* and record your words. Don't worry if you're making any sense; you probably aren't; that's not the point. You are working through your ideas and seeing how they fit.

This is a highly effective way to unblock a draft. I use it all the time. Moving away from your word processor and just walking and speaking means you're no longer in a "writing" mode; you're just talking about ideas. Record them as long as you have stuff to say. Then, return to your desk and transcribe the recording. You may be surprised by how clear your words are.

---

*   *Speaking into your mobilephone is an advantage here because you'll seem less crazy*

In short
1. Copy paste your notes into a blank document
2. Keep you outline design close and use it as a gps
3. Elaborate on your points and clarify the links between ideas
4. Write without a concern for perfection
5. Use generative writing techniques like walk & talk and productive meditation

If you do this, you'll have a first draft, and it's time to move to the last stage of writing: Editing.

Edit

Naturally, your first draft is still rough. A draft is like an evolving design's first model or prototype; the idea is there, but it needs work to function correctly. Editing is the stage where you look closely at your writing and improve it. Imagine fixing up a messy room – you tidy up, throw out things you don't need, and rearrange stuff to make it neater.

Editing is about fixing mistakes, improving sentences, and ensuring everything makes sense. You read through your work, check for errors, and change words or sentences to make them clearer.

You also consider broader, structural issues – does the story flow? Are your ideas organised in a way that makes sense? Editing helps you smooth out the bumps and sharpen your writing. It's the final touches before you show your work to others.

There are two distinct levels of editing, and each one addresses a dimension of the writing process:

Edit
1. Structuring
2. Revision

Structuring

In structural editing, you survey the landscape of your

work, examining the sequence of chapters in a book-length project or the flow of ideas and arguments in a shorter piece. Structural editing concerns the big picture; it isn't about minor tweaks or word choices; it's about the sequence of your thoughts. Picture it as adjusting the structure you laid out in your outline.

We previously discussed how the modular writing approach was like shooting scenes for a film, where you write each section as a coherent text that can be read in isolation and still be meaningful. Well, think of structural editing as the director working in the cutting room, arranging and refining the sequence of scenes. In structural editing, you test the sequence of your writing *scenes*, joining them into a compelling story.

Structural editing operates on the macro level, focusing on the broader picture. It requires eagle-eyed scrutiny of your work to ensure that the sequence of ideas aligns with your outline and conveys your message with impact. For longer works, like a dissertation, structural editing may involve reordering chapters, identifying gaps, or clarifying links between sections. In shorter pieces, editing requires fine-tuning the sequence of paragraphs, ensuring a seamless progression of ideas.

Once your structural foundation is solid and you're satisfied with the sequence of your text, it's time to delve into the craftsmanship of *revision*.

Revision

Until now, the book has focused on demystifying the process of writing. In the editing stage, we look into the *craft* of writing. In other words, how can you write clear, precise, engaging prose that communicates your ideas effectively?

Revision deals with editing your text's words, sentences, and paragraphs. The NODE method of writing generates plenty of content to work with. The method encourages you to notice interesting ideas from your everyday life, be mindful of the media you consume, and gather insights by taking notes. It then pushes you to shape those ideas into longer pieces as drafts. So far, the book has encouraged you to write without a concern for *how* you write. The N–O–D stages covered how to gather and create ideas and get words down on paper so you have material to mould.

The first three stages of the method overcome the myth of the *writer's block* and demystify the writing process because they provide tools to control it and generate compelling content. The NODE method was designed to bring you to this point. If you gathered interesting insights with your **notes**, if you shaped those insights into a unique **outline** that tells a story, and if you expanded your ideas into a rough first **draft**, then it's much easier to shape that material into a sequence of sharp sentences that tell a story.

If you reached this stage, you'll notice how we've come full circle together: remember the *perfect sentence trap*? The perfect sentence trap is the hurdle novice writers struggle to overcome because they invert the NODE process and focus on editing their prose from the start. But if you follow the NODE method, you have material to shape instead of a blank page to despair at.

We have reached the revising stage of the NODE method. Revising can be a daunting task when designers feel blocked and less confident. But there is no reason to be afraid or feel lost. Let's **trust the process** and apply the same principles we applied so far: writing solves a communication problem, and when you choose a particular word, your criteria is to select the most effective word to convey an idea with clarity and precision. That's it. Let that be your guiding principle, and ignore conventions, traditions, or how other people write.

This is the stage when the precision of your prose comes to life. While structural editing deals with the *what* (which ideas to write about) and *where* of your writing (the sequence of those ideas), revising focuses on the *how*: how to write sentences and paragraphs that express your ideas effectively.

Writing sentences while working on a draft demands a free and nonjudgemental mindset; you shouldn't stop midway through a draft to wonder about what you're saying because you will interrupt the flow of ideas. When drafting, don't worry about *form* because you're confident you can revise the text later.

When revising, aim for clarity: choose words that transport an idea from one mind into another without distortion. A tall order, I know. But don't be alarmed. Revising follows particular steps you can learn.

To make this easier, I separated *revision* into the two building blocks of writing: the **sentence** and the **paragraph**. The sentence is the key element of the two. If you can write sentences, you can write paragraphs; the opposite is untrue.

Every idea we have discussed so far converges on the *sentence*. If you can craft compelling sentences, you can write anything.

Part III

Writing Building Blocks

Sentence

Paragraph

I begin to recognise myself, word by word, as I work through a sentence.

Don DeLillo

Sentence

The writer's equation

A sentence is the writer's equation. To solve an equation, you discover how two expressions are connected; to solve a sentence, you discover how words and thoughts are connected. So, writing a sentence is about finding the right shape for a particular thought.

Neither an equation nor a sentence is solved by accident or sudden inspiration, so a writer pores over his sentences like a mathematician solving equations.

The problem, of course, is that thoughts are cloudy. When we introspect to examine our thinking, it often feels like wandering outside on a foggy day. We can just about see outlines and vague shapes, but the details are shrouded. That's because our thoughts are a compound of emotions, memories, images, and words.

So we often find ourselves saying, "I know what I mean, but I can't put it in words," because we can *see* the thought in our mind's eye but struggle to express it with language. Figuring out our thoughts is not straightforward. We try to capture our thinking and make it stand still so we can write it down, but our thoughts resist capture like slippery salmon escaping a hungry bear.

Writing a sentence is more complex than dictating thoughts into a page because words and thoughts are different. This means we cannot solve one side of the equation (the thoughts) to improve the other (the words). We must align both so that thought and language converge into a shape—that shape is a sentence.

Writing, therefore, shapes thought.

Shaping thought

Design is about shaping *things*, writing is about shaping thoughts. Our thinking is meandering, wandering, and wild. It has endless connections and is ill-defined and abstract. Thoughts have no definitive final shape, only a tentative form. Thoughts are like water.

The American actor and martial artist Bruce Lee said in a popular segment of a TV interview that we should be *"like water making its way through cracks. Do not be assertive, but adjust to the object, and you shall find a way around or through it."* The benefits of fluidity are often stated in Eastern philosophies like Buddhism, and Bruce's water analogy also applies to how our thinking works.

Water, like thinking, has no definitive state. It can be *fluid* and meander around ideas without ever settling on a final form; other times, thinking is *vaporous*, like a mist gently enveloping facts, concepts, and ideas; and sometimes thinking *solidifies* into truths, dogmas, or convictions. Solid convictions are harder to change but may again become fluid when a new idea enters our mind like sunburst, melting our beliefs.

Our thinking is malleable and resists being assigned a final shape; thoughts lack rigid boundaries and evolve, shift, and intertwine. No wonder how hard it feels to pin down what we're thinking onto the page.

The first three stages of the NODE method try to capture the richness of our thinking patterns: **notes** follow the principle of idea interconnection, the **outline** sketches the structure supporting those ideas, and the **draft** is the forgiving first attempt to develop ideas on the page. But a first draft is messy, so when **editing** we must order our material into clear and precise prose. That means we must consider each sentence and give it a proper shape.

When we finally shape a sentence, we often realise it's not quite right. So we try again, cut a few words, rewrite others, and read it aloud. We reshape a sentence like a ceramist shaping clay, moulding the words until thought and language become one. So you see, **reshaping our words, in turn, reshapes our thoughts**. And sometimes, when we finally get it right, a sentence surprises us by revealing what we were thinking but couldn't put into words. Writing clarifies our thinking.

We need to give thoughts a temporary shape to understand them. Think of it like the idea of *framing*. Framing is a popular concept in design that describes how designers often make sense of a complex challenge by framing the problem's boundaries. A frame establishes temporary order by defining the limits for experimentation. A sentence is also a frame that defines the temporary limits of a thought.

When we translate thought into words, we can examine our thinking. Writing a sentence reveals if we actually understood a particular topic or idea. Often, we didn't. So, we rewrite and recheck like a mathematician calculating if an equation works. When it does work, a good sentence illuminates our thoughts. It's the exhilarating *aHa!* moment. A sentence feeds the thought back to our mind in a clearer form. By sharpening sentences, we improve our thinking.

In this sense, sentences are a lot like sketches; both externalise our thinking and feed it back into our minds, fueling the creative process. Design Professor Gabriela Goldschmidt describes this iterative process as "the dialectics of sketching;" a similar dialectic occurs when we write a sentence, reflect, and then rewrite it until thought and language click.

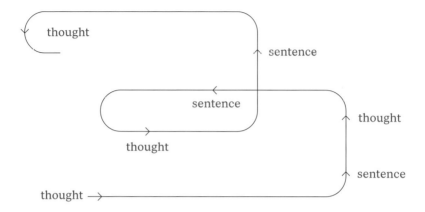

So, the sentence is the basic architecture of writing, with each sentence containing a complete thought. Like architecture organises the spaces where people live, sentences organise the space where thoughts can live. When you write a sentence, you design the house where an idea may dwell and prosper.

Writing a sentence is not what happens after the hard work of thinking is done. Instead, it is the medium of thinking itself. Writing is thinking on paper. Writers must know what meaning they wish to express, but the meaning can only be known by shaping thoughts as sentences; so if you can't put your thoughts into words, you shrink the frontier of your ideas. But the opposite is also true; if you can write, there's no frontier your mind can't reach.

Dead or alive

Sentences can be alive or dead. To the extent they are alive, they are animated by personal human thought. When you examine a sentence, you examine the thought that animates it. But sentences often fall flat. Remember your experience of reading an academic paper filled with empty jargon, such as:

"In order to holistically leverage cutting-edge methodologies and synergise interdisciplinary paradigms, our endeavours are intricately focused on the nuanced exploration and comprehensive examination of multifaceted phenomena."

Or a brand's mission statement buzzword salad:

"Our mission is to empower and inspire by delivering innovative, high-quality services that enhance customer experience. Committed to excellence and sustainability, we strive to exceed expectations through continuous innovation, ethical practices, and a customer-centric approach."

These sentences are dead. They died because they weren't really written by a person but dictated by convention. Jargon, buzzwords, and clichés are typically found in political speeches, marketing and managerial nonsense, and too many academic papers. These are not the product of a personal mind giving considerate thought to his sentences. Rather, these sentences can be pulled out of thin air because they hang over public discourse like smog over a polluted metropolis.

It's also easy. I came up with those two examples in under a minute. That's because there was no thinking involved, just verbal shenanigans. Anyone can write that kind of useless prose, even a computer. The effect it has on the reader is boredom, frustration, and disconnection; there is no human mind reaching another human mind, just nonsense reaching no one.

If you want readers to engage with your sentences, you must first engage your mind while writing them. As you write, aim to get an idea as precisely as possible out of your mind into your reader's*. So, ask yourself: *What am I trying to say? What words express it clearly? Can it be shorter? Does this point need an example?* And so on.

Or you can ignore all this trouble, turn off your mind, and let convention craft your sentences for you. But realise that ready-made sentences are the old thinking of someone else; they may contain residues of what was once an exciting idea, but their original flavour is lost like a delicious meal reheated in a microwave oven.

Here are a couple more examples: *"The world is changing,"* which is a cliché, or *"in the pedagogical milieu of juvenile cognitive development, the synergistic amalgamation of ludic engagement and didactic stimuli propels the heuristic acquisition of knowledge by infants**"* which is jargon for *"Children learn while playing."* These sentences are the product of automatic thinking; words empty of meaning, like a zombie is empty of life.

Here's the issue: zombie sentences do not aim to communicate at all. For instance, the aim of many jargon-filled academic papers is not to communicate new knowledge but to advance a professor's career; an internal memo by an HR department may have the goal of being as unclear as possible for legal reasons; a political statement often aims to divert responsibility, like the classic "mistakes were made" uttered by countless politicians after a tragedy. These are not good examples if your goal is to reach another person's mind.

---

* *I know this is an impossible task, but it's an ideal worth pursuing*
** *Don't laugh, as a professor I read sentences like that constantly*

The goal of a sentence is to show the reader something the writer has noticed. It could be an abstract idea like *"Design is the craft of creating beautifully useful things"* or a concrete idea like *"A door shouldn't have a handle if you push to open."* Sentences should show something to the reader. But the writer is not just describing things. The writer presents them.

Sentences and presentation

A sentence is a window to the world, not a mirror to the self.

Writing should reveal something new about the world, not something personal about the writer. Unless, of course, you're writing about yourself. But even in that case, a sentence shouldn't call attention to itself. Readers shouldn't notice sentences any more than they notice the windowpane when looking outside.

When writing, you *show* the reader something you noticed. A helpful analogy is a conversation: think about writing like walking in a park with a friend when you notice the birdsong of a nightingale and guide your friend to listen. You don't lecture her about birds nor dramatise how it makes you feel; you point her attention towards the song so she may hear it, too.

In Psychology, this is called *joint attention*: when two people coordinate their attention towards the same thing. It's easy to do in person but much harder in writing. When writing, you're *talking* with an imaginary reader that never responds, what Prof. Maryanne Wolf calls an "attentive ghost". Novice writers often forget they are *talking* with the reader, and their prose collapses into abstractions they would never use in a conversation.

But you remember the conversation analogy while you write. In that case, the reader will feel personally addressed, not lectured at, nor the innocent target of a bombardment of platitudes, jargon, and abstractions. A conversation relies on simple language and a genuine effort to communicate ideas. Professors Thomas and Turner suggest writers should imagine a *scene* where the reader and writer are present and capable of noticing the same things.

While writing, pretend that the reader is there with you, paying attention to something both can notice, like a nightingale chirping on a tree. The purpose of writing is to present something interesting you also want a friend (the attentive ghost) to notice. This mindset places the reader front and centre, much like designing places the user's needs at the forefront of a project. In design, the user is always right. If the user doesn't understand your design, your design fails. If a reader doesn't understand your writing, your writing fails, too.

Presentation must be clear, but presentation is not a dry description. A plain description of some fact about the world is different from *presenting* an idea. When you present an idea, you choose what matters and ignore the rest. You want your friend to notice the birdsong while walking in the park, so everything else must recede into the background: other people's chatter, aeroplanes flying by, the trees, and the flowers, all hush like an orchestra before a violin solo.

The NODE method comes full circle. The writing journey begins when you *notice* something interesting and ends when the reader notices the same thing too. The presentation is clear, like a window opening to the world. A good sentence should feel inevitable as if no other sequence of words would do. **Form** (the words) and **function** (the meaning) meld into a sentence that carries an idea from one mind into another.

A good sentence appears **clear** and **precise** like a correct equation.

Easier said than done, or poor sentences wouldn't abound. What makes a good sentence? How do you write one? And is there a particular structure to a good sentence? Yes, there is. A design lurks behind every good sentence.

Let's examine how it works.

How to design
a sentence

Let's start with the basic definition of a sentence and take it from there.

A sentence is a sequence of words that contains a subject and a predicate and expresses a complete thought.

So every sentence must have:
1. The subject
2. The predicate

The **subject** is what the sentence is about. It is typically a noun, pronoun, or noun phrase that performs an action or is being described. For instance:

She is reading a book.

"She" is the subject of the sentence because the pronoun "she" is performing the action, which is reading.

The **predicate** consists of a verb and any accompanying information that describes what the subject is doing or what is happening in the sentence. For instance, in the example above "is reading a book" is the predicate.

Subject and predicate are the bedrock of any sentence. I promised this book wouldn't bore you with grammar, so here's another way to think about it: good sentences express a clear **action** you can attribute to an **actor** (someone or some thing).

Sentence Blueprint

Actor (subject) + Action (predicate)

The actor + action formula is the foundation of any sentence. I like to call it the **sentence blueprint**. Richard Lanham, an American literary scholar, said that a good way to remember the basic blueprint of a sentence is to identify *who kicked whom*. Roy Peter Clark, a renowned writing coach, suggests memorising *who kicked the dog*, and author Joe Moran describes the formula as *doer, done, done to*. Same thing; these templates highlight that a sentence is always about **someone doing something** (often to someone else).

But, does the sentence blueprint apply only to people? No. An actor could be anything, for instance:

The Beatles *performed live at the Royal Albert Hall*

Society *is unfair*

The Universe *is expanding*

The Universe is expanding is a perfect example of a sentence following the **sentence blueprint**. The Universe is the **actor** performing the **action** of expanding. It's also an excellent example of expressing a complex idea using simple language. When writing a sentence, spell out the action and who performed it; if you do, the meaning of your sentences will be clear. And clarity is critical for effective communication.

To write clear sentences, you should consider **verbs** closely. Verbs describe the action in a sentence, and when used well, they support the writer in precision and expressiveness. For instance:

John worked very hard on his book, is worse than

John **struggled** *with his book.*

The verb to *struggle* shortened the sentence by two words. Struggle is also sharper than "worked very hard". When revising, I spend ages hunting the right verbs. But it pays off.

So, always be clear on who's acting and chose a strong verb that describes the action:

John **wrote** *a book.*

The government **raised** *taxes.*

Social media companies **harvest** *their users' attention.*

Apple trees **bear** *fruit in late Summer.*

A group of astronomers **spotted** *a meteorite heading towards Earth.*

ACTOR	ACTION
John	write
The goverment	raise
Social media companies	harvest
Apple trees	bear
A group of astronomers	spot

Strong **active** verbs energise sentences. The opposite leads to **passive** constructions like:

The book was read by Susan.

In a passive sentence construction (or *passive voice*), the subject is the recipient of the action rather than the doer. Instead of an actor doing something, we get a vague impression that something occurred without it being obvious who did what to whom.

What's worse is that often, there is no one acting at all in the passive sentence. The actor evaporates, and something just happens without a cause:

Taxes were raised.

The report was reviewed.

A final decision about the application was made.

As you can see, no one is raising, reviewing, or deciding. The third sentence above is particularly egregious because if you analyse it, it doesn't tell you anything at all. Who decided? And what was the decision anyway? If we revise the sentence using the sentence blueprint, we get the much clearer:

The review board rejected the application.

Passive construction shines if you aim to divert responsibility, obscure meaning, and confuse your readers. But if you aim for clear communication, to reach your reader's mind effectively, to engage with your reader, stick with the active voice.

There are exceptions, of course. Sometimes we need to spot-light the object of the action, rather than the actor:

The new intern was hired by Jane.

The emphasis of the sentence above is on the intern, not Jane. A mindful writer will know when to adopt the passive voice if it contributes to conveying the message effectively. A writer in automatic mode will mindlessly revert to the passive because that's the *sound* of what's out there.

Here's the deal: the problem is not the passive voice itself. We have a problem when the passive voice turns into the default writing mode, an automatic style adopted carelessly. The automatic writing style tends towards the bureaucratic, the obscure, and the convoluted.

What's worse, passive sentence construction invites its friends along for the ride: abstraction, jargon, and verbiage, galloping like the four horsemen of terrible writing, waging war on clarity. And so we get sentences like

The utilisation of intricate terminology in a manner that lacks conciseness and embraces unnecessary elaboration was observed, as the document underwent a process of examination by the reviewing committee.

As you can see, passive sentences hit you like a tranquiliser dart. Notice the weak verbs ending on "–ion" (utilisa*tion*, elabora*tion*, examina*tion*) and the actor buried under layers of abstract and convoluted language, gasping for air. By the time we meet the actors (the reviewing committee), we're unsure of what the heck is going on. Who kicked whom?

The antidote is the good sentence blueprint: identify the actor and place it at the beginning, identify the action and turn it into an active verb (examine, find), cut verbiage ("the process of examination" turns into *examined*), and we get:

> *The reviewing committee examined the document*
> *and found it wordy and jargon heavy.*

It's not Nobel prize-winning prose, but it's clear.

Here's a famous example of passive sentences. The American general Dwight Eisenhower allegedly asked Winston Churchill to review a draft of a speech he'd written. Eisenhower's speech was long and abstruse. After reading it, Churchill reprimanded Eisenhower for writing convoluted sentences filled with abstract verbs like "systematise", "prioritise", and "finalise". The British war hero drove the point home when he asked Eisenhower, "What if I had said, instead of *we shall fight on the beaches, Hostilities will be engaged with our adversary on the coastal perimeter*"?

Churchill's *We shall fight on the beaches* depicts a Britain on the attack. It's part of a speech that inspired a whole nation to face fearful odds. On the contrary, *Hostilities will be engaged with our adversary on the coastal perimeter* is the language of a timid bureaucrat filling in a tax deduction form. It inspires no one.

Churchill's speech famously closes with "We shall never surrender"; imagine if instead, it would have ended with "appeasement with our adversary will be declined." You get the point.

We shall fight on the beaches follows the good sentence blueprint to the letter; its simplicity is astounding:

ACTOR	ACTION
We	fight

Locating the actor in *hostilities will be engaged with our adversary on the coastal perimeter*, on the contrary, is hard work. And I wonder what the action is supposed to be. "Engaging," perhaps? Who knows. Also, what images does *coastal perimeter* evoke to the reader? None. *Beaches*, on the other hand, connect tangibly with the reader's mind, evoking memories, emotions, or stills from the invasion on D-day.

Sadly, we too often read the "Hostilities will be engaged with our adversary" kind of claptrap. It's everywhere. It's so common across industries that Richard Lanham calls it "the official style". The official style capitalises on passive voice and convoluted, wordy sentences empty of content. This style is ubiquitous in academia, political speeches, and corporate speak. It's so widespread it's like elevator music played quietly and continuously in public places to make people feel bored. So, naturally, a novice writer will unconsciously reproduce that sound when writing, the sound of the official style: long, bureaucratic, and dull.

Churchill's powerful rhetoric is a more helpful example than the drab language of the official style; comparing both illustrates the value of good sentence design for clear communication. Good sentences use simple language to engage and inspire. Simplicity is powerful. *We shall fight on the beaches* is simpler than *hostilities will be engaged*. But Churchill is saying something extraordinary using ordinary language anyone can understand.

Not all passive sentences are wrong, but poor writing

often stems from passive construction. Avoid it. Start with someone doing something. Active constructions that follow the sentence blueprint are shorter, direct, easier to understand, and more engaging. Use the passive voice sparingly. The *active voice* is a more solid foundation for your sentences.

Good sentences

Good writers electrify their sentences with powerful verbs, like *fight*. Not with pompous prose stuffed with nonsense like "incentivising frameworks of innovative synergies" (I once read this gem on a brand's mission statement).

And yet, our first drafts are often filled with passive sentences because it's so steeped in the public discourse that we replicate them without noticing. No matter. Editing is mostly about *revising* the sentences you wrote in the first draft. When we apply the good sentence blueprint to a sentence, we spotlight its meaning. But often, the meaning falls short. For instance:

A decision was made by the project manager.

Let's see if we can improve it. The actor is obviously the project manager, and the action is to decide, which gives us: *The project manager decided.* But this sentence is odd. Decided *what*? And who is the "project manager" anyway?

Revising this sentence by applying the good sentence blueprint rendered its meaninglessness obvious. But now that the sentence's emptiness is in full display, we can improve it:

Claire decided to postpone the project.

We now have a clearer idea of what's going on, the project was postponed, and who postponed it? Claire. The fact that she's the project manager is implied or can be stated in a previous or subsequent sentence; for instance *As the project manager, Claire decides when the project kicks off.*

Let's revise further. The action is not really Claire's *decision*, is it? It's the *postponing* of the project, so we can eliminate the word *decide*.

> *Claire postponed the project.*

But isn't "the project" too generic? What project are we talking about?

> *Claire postponed the horizon initiative.*

I know, "the horizon initiative" is a terrible name for a project, but I'm trying to keep the example realistic. We can add a bit more detail if we write:

> *Claire postponed the horizon*
> *initiative until next Spring.*

That's a fine sentence. It clearly conveys information, the actor doing the action is easy to spot, and it ends with the lovely word *Spring*. We could've written "the next quarter" instead of "Spring", but where *next quarter* is bureaucratic, *Spring* is evocative.

You can build more complex sentences out of the actor + action structure. As long as you have a solid actor + action foundation, you can make your sentences as long or short as you like. Here's an example of longer sentences that follow the blueprint:

> *John wrote an insightful article during*

his Christmas holiday.

Data from the Hubble telescope shows the Universe
has been expanding since the big bang.

The **sentence blueprint** makes any sentence modular. For example:

John wrote a book.

You can take the basic blueprint and add to it without compromising on clarity:

John wrote a book about design during
the Christmas break.

You can expand as much as you want when the actor + action is placed at the start of a sentence because the reader never loses track of *who did what*:

John wrote a book about design during the Christmas break;
he had been researching it for a while and was pleased to
finally finding the time to finish it.

When you master the actor + action blueprint, you can explore a third element called **the sentence knockout**.

Sentence knockouts

A sentence knockout is any word or short phrase that closes a sentence with a bang. Roy Peter Clark describes these words as *hitting the target*. The goal is to identify special words you want to spotlight and move them to the end of the sentence. Any idea that precedes the full stop will get special attention from your reader.

The classic example of a sentence knockout comes from Shakespeare's play "Macbeth". Macbeth's servant enters the scene with the tragic news of the death of Lady Macbeth and says:

> *The Queen, my lord, is dead.*

Roy Peter Clark points out that the conventional way to write the sentence would be *The queen is dead my lord*. But Shakespeare was not a conventional writer. He knew that placing a word at the end of a sentence dramatically enhances its significance.

If you think sentence knockouts are just for dramatic plays and Shakespeare, I give you evolutionary biologist Richard Dawkins explaining the remarkably low probability of a person's existence:

> *The potential people who could have been here in my place but who will in fact never see the light of day outnumber the sand grains of Arabia.*

The phrase *the sand grains of Arabia* elevates a dry point about probability. It makes Dawkins's prose come alive. It's an effective analogy that helps the reader understand a complex idea.

Closing a sentence with a special word or phrase will increase its impact. The sentence will linger on the reader's memory like a punchline from a joke. Or, indeed, like a knockout punch to the face.

Knockouts make sentences memorable. But there's more; remember how we discussed that the human mind is always eager to make sense? When the reader lands on a word that hits the target and drives a point home, the sentence–sometimes a whole paragrah–is suddenly illuminated. The reader **wants** it to make sense.

The complctc good sentence blueprint looks like this::

$$Actor + Action \times (knockout)$$

The knockout follows a multiplication sign because it multiplies a sentence's meaning. Use the knockout sparingly, or you'll exhaust the reader. And for full effect, knockouts are better placed at the end of a paragraph.

Join sentences with an invisible thread.

Joe Moran

Paragraph

Before the first word processor, writers typed their drafts on a typewriter. When drafting, it was common to leave a gap between each paragraph. The writer would then slice up every paragraph with scissors, turning his draft into a stack of slips of paper, each containing a single paragraph. Then, he would rearrange the paragraphs into a new order and paste them on a blank piece of paper. After that, the writer would retype the new draft and start over.

Now you know where the expression *cut and paste* comes from. And also why the icon for *cut* remains a pair of scissors on most word processors. Luckily for us, the cut-and-paste commands on a computer turned this painstaking procedure into a couple of clicks. Some writers, like prolific journalist John McPhee, still print out their drafts and cut the paragraphs by hand using scissors. Sometimes, when there's enough time, I do this too, and there's a strange satisfaction from playing with physical slips of paper that you just don't get from moving text around on a word processor.

This story illustrates a key point about writing: paragraphs are independent units of meaning that can be rearranged like bricks. Sounds familiar? We discussed how an effective writing process is *modular*. We learned how to break a large writing assignment into single sections written in isolation and recombined. And how notes are small vessels of meaning we can use and re-use. And how each sentence is the home for a specific thought. The writing process is modular at all levels of analysis.

So, naturally, paragraphs are modular too. Paragraphs are coherent units of meaning, as flexible as Lego blocks. Think of paragraphs as the **building blocks** of your text. You stack them up into a shape; if you're unhappy, you can throw them on the floor and start over.

Modular paragraphs smooth the way for editing your text. You focus on making each paragraph coherent and cohesive so you can rearrange their sequence according to the story you're telling. Obviously, the sequence should have an inner logic, an invisible thread holding the narrative together.

To do this, you must *design* your paragraphs so they fit together, like Lego blocks that always fit on top of other blocks. Paragraph blocks improve the readability of your text like a well-designed interface improves the usability of a product.

The modular paragraph

The ideal paragraph consists of **one point**. In writing, a *point* is the main idea or message you want to convey; it's the focus of a paragraph. A paragraph should revolve around a single, clear idea. The point of a paragraph can be an argument, a claim, an idea, or any central theme that ties together the supporting details.

Having one point per paragraph clarifies your writing. It allows readers to follow your argument or narrative without being overwhelmed by multiple ideas stuffed into a paragraph, like clowns inside a beatle in a circus act. Paragraphs are more like a university student's dorm room: there's just enough space for **one** student to sleep in, store his stuff, and study. A dorm room may accommodate a couple of students, but it's a stretch. More than two students and you have a rowdy party in a tight space; fun, perhaps, but you end up dazed and confused.

Same with paragraphs. Cram too many ideas into a paragraph, and you confuse your reader. Ideas, like people, need room to breathe. Too often, novice writers don't allow enough space for their ideas to grow and develop. A paragraph should expand on a point, carefully detailing its contours so the reader can see what you mean. **A good paragraph introduces a point, tells the reader why she should care, and closes by driving the point home**.

So, how do you construct a paragraph?

First, ignore any hard and fast rules about a specific number of sentences. It's unclear if the ideal paragraph should have one, five, or ten sentences. A paragraph should make a point; sometimes, the point fits into a single sentence. More often, you need a few sentences to make a point. As a rule of thumb, aim for six to ten sentences per paragraph, then occasionally write more or less than that ballpark number. A paragraph with more than ten sentences will likely make more than a single point.

Each paragraph is a unit of meaning. Group related sentences into paragraphs that elaborate on the same point. Let your sentences be drawn to a paragraph like metal to a magnet. This makes your paragraphs easier to read and boosts the impact of your writing. Armed with the guiding principle of *one point per paragraph* you can design your paragraphs as modules you can swap into any sequence.

You follow the sentence blueprint to write good sentences; you can also follow a blueprint to build good paragraphs. I have two paragraph templates I like to use:

1. The three-act paragraph
2. The academic cavalry charge

The first is a general paragraph structure for any type of writing. A versatile structure that can accomodate any writing purpose. The second is a variation you may need for academic writing.

The three-act paragraph

Things structured in *threes* have a supernatural inner coherence. You find it everywhere. There are three time periods: Past, Present, and Future; three primary colours: Red, Blue, and Yellow; three stages in life: Birth, Life, and Death; three processes in computing: Input, Processing, and Output; and music is organised into Melody, Harmony, and Rhythm. The rule of three works, so let's use it to structure our paragraphs.

The three-act structure is often used to tell stories, particularly films and plays. Classic storytelling splits the narrative into Setup, Confrontation, and Resolution. This narrative framework guides audiences through a journey that captivates with a strong beginning, intensifies with conflict, and reaches a satisfying resolution.

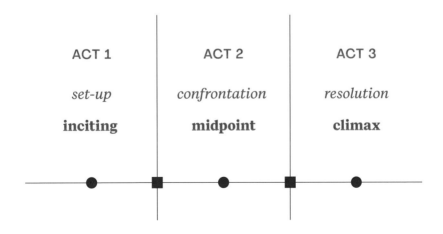

We can use similar principles to structure our paragraphs as if each paragraph were a micro-story with a beginning, middle, and end. From this point of view, the stages of a paragraph are:

1. **Opener**: a sentence that introduces the point of the paragraph

2. **Build-up**: a series of sentences expanding and explaining the point

3. **Closure**: a sentence that drives the point home

The paragraph opener

In a film, a play, or a novel, Act One is the exposition or setup. It describes the main characters, their setting, and explores the world they live in. In other words, Act One is an introduction to the story that's about to unfold. So, how can you introduce a paragraph? A paragraph concerns *one point*, so open a paragraph by introducing the point you're about to make.

There are, of course, several ways to introduce the same point. A one-sentence paragraph opener is ideal, but that sentence may take many shapes. The opener is the **hook**; its purpose is to explain the paragraph, captivate the reader and lure her into the text.

Whether you're writing an extended or short piece, vary the *type* of paragraph opener. Not only its shape but also its **intensity**. The first paragraph of a section, chapter, dissertation, or book differs from the 12th paragraph midway through a chapter.

Types of paragraph openers

Imagine you're making a point about design and smartphone usage. Let's consider different types of opener:

Question A question is a great way to start a paragraph. It immediately attracts the reader's curiosity because she will want to know the answer. Start with a question if you want an immediate hook. Act One in a story usually raises a *dramatic question*, "Will they get married?", "Can they find the lost temple?" or "Who murdered the cook?". But beware of too many questions, or the reader will feel like she's taking a test.

Examples:

> *Are smartphones destroying our attention spans?*

> *Can we redesign smartphones to help people reclaim their focus?*

Claim: A strong, declarative statement directly expressing the writer's main point. When you open with a claim, you state the idea you're about to develop in that paragraph. A claim can be bold and attention-grabbing; it makes a clear, assertive statement that sets the tone for the rest of the paragraph. For that reason, claims are powerful chapter or article openers.

> *Smartphones are destroying our attention spans.*

> *Smartphone distraction is not a bug; it's a design feature.*

Topic Sentence: A topic sentence is similar to a claim but neutrally introduces the paragraph's main idea. The topic sentence outlines the subject of the paragraph without presenting a personal argument. It's a guide for the reader, indicating what the paragraph will be about. A claim is bold, direct, and opinionated. A topic sentence is more neutral

Smartphones have an impact on our attention spans.

Call to Action: A Call to Action inspires the reader to take a specific action or respond in a particular way. A call to action makes an impactful opener for an article or book.

Design should help people regain control over their attention spans.

Problem: Open with a problem to highlight a potential issue or drawback. Stating a problem is similar to a topic sentence; the difference is that stating a problem focuses on the problematic aspects of the topic. The tone is objective and analytical.

The impact of smartphones on our ability to focus is a growing concern.

Solution: Invert the reader's expectation and open with a solution to address an issue. Opening a paragraph with a solution *assumes* there is a problem that needs to be addressed.

Let's design better ways to use smartphones and help people reclaim their focus.

Anecdote: Share a short story or anecdote to capture the reader's attention and wrap your point around a human concern. An anecdote is effective because it's relatable. Your reader will resonate from similar experiences or understand yours. Anecdotes are impactful ways to introduce a topic but should be used sparingly. Also, an anecdote is often longer than a single sentence.

A few weeks ago, my 7-year old scored a goal in football practice. But I didn't see it, a buzzing notification lowered my eyesight just as the ball hit the back of the net. The heartbreak in his eyes will haunt me forever.

Citation: Open with a relevant quote to lend authority or add an insightful perspective to your opening.

"In an age of constant distraction, it's not the interruption that matters most; it's how we choose to respond" – Nir Eyal

Statistic: Present a compelling statistic to emphasise the significance of your topic. Facts and statistics are often buried in the body of a paragraph, not the opener. But you can open with an impactful fact to spotlight a vital issue of your point.

The average person checks their smartphone over 150 times a day; that's once every six minutes.

These openers address the same point from a slightly different angle. The opener of the first paragraph in a piece should be memorable and set the tone for what follows. For a regular paragraph, the opener's function is to hook the reader and entice her to read on. The paragraph opener guides the reader; it should tell her something she doesn't know or surprise her with a fresh perspective on a topic. So, make the opener as sharp as you can.

The type of opener determines where the paragraph's build-up goes. The build-up should answer the **question**, present evidence for the **claim**, elaborate on the **topic**, support the **solution**, describe the **problem**, elaborate why the **anecdote** or **citation** is meaningful, and so on.

Build-up

The opener introduced your point. Now it's time to show why it matters. The build-up presents details, evidence, examples, analogies, arguments, or other elements supporting and deepening your point. Staying with our example, let's see where the paragraph goes:

Smartphones are destroying our attention spans.
The average person checks their smartphone over 150 times
daily, once every six minutes. No wonder people can't
focus on anything for longer than, well, six minutes or so.
It's now common to witness friends and family glued to their
screens during meals or conversations, or worse, couples
hooked on their phones during a date. This is not a bug; it's
a design feature. Features like push notifications, swipe-to-
refresh, or infinite scroll are designed to capture users'
attention and not let go.

Again, the paragraph above may not win the Pulitzer Prize, but it gets the message across. It introduces the point and presents *reasons* why you should care. It alludes to broader issues (digital technology and human relationships) without losing track of the main point. The sentences work together to deliver the main point. But how do we weave sentences inside a paragraph?

There are three guidelines you can follow to combine sentences inside a paragraph. These guidelines are designed to improve clarity and engage with the reader's mind. The guidelines build on the idea that writing is a conversation with an *attentive ghost*, a friend (real or imaginary) that you address. This imaginary conversation sets up a human tone. It takes work, but the reader will thank you.

Guideline 1 *Climb from the particular to the general*

When writing, move from the particular to the general, not vice versa. Anchor your writing in words the reader can see in her mind's eye. To do this, author Jefferson Bates suggests we never lose track of the *ladder of abstraction*.

The same words may have different meanings. People constantly disagree on definitions and on what concepts a word is pointing to. It's sensible, therefore, to always define your terms when you use an abstract word. An even better strategy is to climb your way towards the abstract term. Begin by establishing a common ground with your reader using concrete words. Use words that trigger a mental image.

The Ladder of Abstraction

Abstract or General ↑	Living organisms
	Animals
	Vertebrates
	Mammals
	Canines
	Dogs
	German Shepherd
Concrete or Specific ↓	Max

Ascending the ladder, each word grows more abstract than the one below. Also, each term grows vague and conceptual. "Max" is someone's pet dog. "Living organisms" represent all biological life. Abstract terms are nearly impossible to visualise because they summon no concrete images to the reader's mind.

The lower steps are concrete terms readers can see, feel, or imagine while reading. These are *things* any person has experienced, so they represent standard terms anyone can understand. Recall our example from before:

We shall fight them on the beaches

and

Hostilities will be engaged with our adversary on the coastal perimeter

We can picture a beach but struggle to interpret "coastal perimeter". A concrete term helps the reader keep her pace while reading instead of stopping to wonder what *coastal perimeter* actually means. Abstract terms tax the reader's attention and force her to stop. Too many abstract terms in a row, and you lose your reader's interest. Abstract, vague, general terms are more verbal; they engage the part of our brain that deals with verbal language. Concrete terms, in contrast, fully engage the reader's mind because they activate our memories, sensory gears, and emotions.

Don't misunderstand me. **Abstract terms are fundamental**; we couldn't reason appropriately without them. Academics, for instance, rely on abstractions to develop theories that describe complex issues. But, when writing, the best scholars present their theories with examples or illustrations that link abstractions to concrete things the reader can grasp.

Richard Feynman won the Nobel Prize in Physics for his breakthroughs in quantum electrodynamics. Physics is a complex topic to grasp, perhaps the hardest. But Feynman was a remarkable teacher, with the rare ability to explain physics in a way anyone could understand. He famously said, *"it is natural to explain new ideas in terms of what is already in your own head"*. His lectures and books were filled with examples and analogies that illustrated ideas like the force of gravity.

To understand a problem or a new concept or idea, Feynman would try to write it down in simple terms. The goal was to see if he could explain it so that a clever teenager would understand it. Whether he was figuring out how the force of gravity interacts with light or the shape of a black hole, Feynman would force himself to write it down in the simplest possible language. When he could explain a complex thing by writing it in simple terms, he knew he understood it completely.

If you're writing a paragraph about an abstract topic, use the ladder of abstraction to guide the reader from something she can grasp towards a more general idea. For instance, imagine you're writing about *interaction*. Interaction is a key process in design, but it's also a vague concept covering many people's experiences with things. You can start by describing simpler activities familiar to anyone, like opening a door or using the ATM, and move upwards to a broader understanding of interaction.

Your paragraph build-up should climb towards higher levels of abstraction, not the other way around. Anchor your ideas on concrete things people already know from experience. And never use abstractions needlessly. Don't write "engaging in ambulatory activities contributes positively to physical fitness" when you mean "Walking is healthy".

If you explain something complex in simple terms, your reader feels smart. Anyone can complicate a subject; only someone who understands can simplify it. So, explain extraordinary things in ordinary words. A complex topic requires simple language to understand.

Keep your sentences clear and simple, with concrete terms and active verbs. Now, how do you join sentences together?

Guideline 2 *signposting*

Novice writers, eager to appear competent and in control, often build their paragraphs with the support of verbal crutches. So their sentences are joined by transitional words such as *additionally, furthermore, moreover, consequently, therefore, nonetheless, however, nevertheless, in conclusion* and so on.

These words spell out the relationships between sentences. But beware, like abstract terms, use them sparingly. Transitional words are verbal signposts that guide the reader, like road signs on a highway. But with too much verbal signposting, the reader slowly enters a verbal mindset and turns off the emotional, sensory, and visual parts of her mind.

Instead, write good sentences following the sentence blueprint and join them subtly inside a paragraph. Rely on short sentences connected with humble conjunctions like "and," "but," "so", and "or". This creates a straightforward narrative, moving your paragraphs with a natural flow. The movement and flow you also find in a good conversation.

You don't need excessive signposting when your paragraph is locked at both ends by a sentence opener and closure. The sentences work together naturally, like a balanced colour palette. Signposting overrides your writing voice, and the conversation with the attentive reader turns into a one-way lecture.

A paragraph's sentences are kept together by the invisible sinews of meaning. Trust the reader's intelligence to grasp subtle relationships between sentences. This writing style creates a natural *build-up* towards the paragraph's ending, a sense of growing expectation you also feel when reading a good story.

Guideline 3 *less is more*

As a general rule, avoid verbiage. Clarity goes hand in hand with simplicity, so prefer short words to longer ones and keep your sentences short. But like there is no hard and fast rule for the number of sentences in a paragraph, sentence length can vary. A long sentence can be clear and precise and contain no needless words.

In a paragraph, long sentences work so long as they lean on short ones. And vice-versa. Too many consecutive short sentences create an unpleasant start-and-stop rhythm, like a car stuck in a traffic jam. But too many long sentences exhaust your reader's cognitive energy. Vary the length of your sentences to make your writing more lively and expressive. Like in an interesting piece of music, the cadence matters. Shorter sentences stand out if they follow a longer one. Believe me.

So, move from the particular to the general, avoid signposting, and vary sentence length to make your writing more expressive. Your paragraph is building up to a close. Now what?

Closure

The paragraph closure should drive your point home. Your build-up creates momentum and movement towards the end. You've presented reasons the reader should care, but the closure seals the deal.

Like a strong opener is better saved for the first paragraph in a piece, the strong closure should be reserved for the final one. It's a matter of managing the intensity of your writing. Any paragraph should have a strong opener and closure, but you must vary their intensity. If each paragraph opens and closes with a bold statement, your writing will appear strident and lacking nuance.

Manage your strongest lines carefully, like an artist playing with colour accents to emphasise meaning in a painting. The paragraph closure should offer a satisfying resolution for your point and build a bridge for the next one. When revising paragraphs, you can tweak paragraph closures to form links with the following paragraph to keep the reader interested.

Some types of paragraph openers are also good closures. For instance, you can close a paragraph with a question, causing a *cliffhanger* effect on your reader. But remember that questions in prose are like changing gears in a car; they give your text a sudden boost. So, don't end every paragraph with a question (especially if you opened with one), or you end up overwhelming the reader.

You can also end your paragraph with a **sentence knockout** to drive the point home. Sentence knockouts are perfect for wrapping up a paragraph because the full stop, followed by the blank space, invites the reader to stop and take in the point.

The three-act paragraph invites the reader to join the discussion of a topic. It takes on a conversational tone. These paragraphs require space and a slow pace, where each point takes as long as necessary to present, elaborate, and conclude.

The three act paragraph

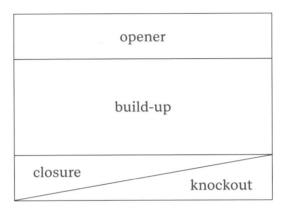

But sometimes, time and space are short, and you must make a series of complex points using fewer words, like in an academic paper. Or you want to drive a point home beyond dispute. On these occasions, we summon the cavalry.

The academic cavalry charge

In a cavalry charge, the rider leading the onslaught was often called the *point* or the *point man*. The *point* described the person at the forefront of a galloping force. The knight leading the charge set the pace and direction of the attack, and his role was essential for the success of the strike.

A cavalry charge didn't get a second chance to break the enemy lines. It either worked and hit a decisive blow that turned a battle around, or it dispersed, and the knights were picked up one by one by their enemies. The academic argument is just like a cavalry charge, only slightly less bloody.

Academic arguments must be packed into tight paragraphs that do not fail to hit their targets. An academic point must be followed by a robust charge of arguments, facts, examples, and evidence. Often in as few words as possible because of word count constraints. Not an easy feat.

When writing for academia, or whenever space is short and a point is crucial, you may alternate the three-act paragraph with the academic cavalry charge. The academic cavalry charge allows you to make a complex point using fewer words. The structure is also divided into three parts. But, where the three-act paragraph welcomes variation, the three parts of the academic cavalry charge remain the same.

Academic cavalry charge structure

- **Point**: a topic sentence or claim stating the point
- **Charge**: a host of evidence supporting the point
- **Hit the target**: wrap-up sentence concluding the point

Point

The opener for the academic paragraph must be straightforward. It can be either a topic sentence stating the main idea or a claim asserting an idea without hesitation. This sentence defines the direction of your paragraph; it can't afford to be ambiguous or unclear. The effect on the reader can't be lukewarm. It's better for the reader to disagree with you than to remain indifferent. Remember, a reader who disagrees with you is engaging with your words.

Your reader will expect reasons to support your opening claim. And the bolder the claim, the heavier the expectation. Keep in mind the advice popularised by the astronomer Carl Sagan that *"extraordinary claims require extraordinary evidence."* So, marshal your best evidence, and have it follow your point like horsemen galloping into battle.

Charge

The supporting sentences are crucial in an academic paragraph; they drive the charge that follows the opening claim. After asserting the main idea with the topic sentence, the supporting sentences follow up with evidence, examples, or details to strengthen the argument.

Supporting sentences present evidence or facts that back up the main point. The evidence is drawn from published academic studies, reports, or historical events. Look for compelling facts, well-established research, and other arguments from respected scholars.

The charge should also elaborate on the initial point by providing context, offering specific details, or explaining why the evidence is significant. These paragraphs tend to run longer than the six to ten sentences suggested before. But be careful not to overwhelm the reader. A massive twenty-sentence block may intimidate your reader into skimming or skipping your paragraph. This is the opposite of what you want. You want to convince your reader with reasons, not bore her into submission.

Each sentence adds a reason for accepting the initial claim as true or valid. The information provided by these sentences adds up to build a compelling argument. The charge is made by sentence after sentence in a relentless rhetorical push like horsemen breaking through enemy lines.

If done well, the academic cavalry charge doesn't need a sentence knock-out. The charge provides enough evidence and context to fortify the initial claim. Yet, the paragraph can be wrapped up with a sentence that restates the initial claim in light of the evidence.

Hit the target

The academic cavalry charge doesn't meander; it's a precise strike designed to hit the target dead centre. In this final act, you must wrap up the paragraph by reiterating the main point in light of the presented evidence. Imagine you're delivering the decisive blow in a jousting match – accuracy and impact matter.

The hit-the-target sentence is your chance to leave a lasting impression. Make it clear and concise, emphasising how the evidence supports and reinforces the initial claim. This sentence should resonate with the reader, leaving her with a solid understanding of why your point is valid and compelling.

Remember, it's not about introducing new information; it's about summarising the evidence and restating the main idea in a way that lingers in the reader's mind. The hit-the-target sentence should be the exclamation point at the end of your paragraph, leaving no doubt about the strength of your argument—only a field of victory.

Academic cavalry charge

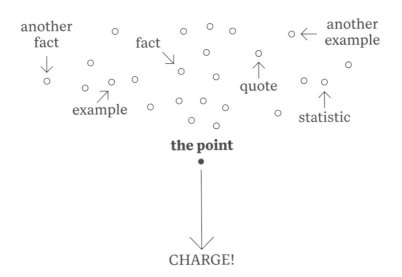

Note   # Outline

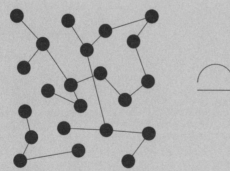   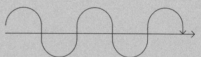

Draft

Edit

I have spent most of the day putting in a comma and the rest of the day taking it out.

Attributed to Oscar Wilde

Reclaim your mind

I'm not the first person to notice that our lives are accelerating. Everything goes faster, we expect things immediately, and everybody is busy.

What are we busy with? Emails downpour our inboxes, notifications explode on our screens like fireworks, and meetings squeeze into our calendars like pieces in a Tetris game. And every message, of course, is labelled "urgent." Meanwhile, the hard work of creating ideas and shaping them into reality, the work that matters, hibernates.

Everybody knows the work they should be doing or wish they did but don't. That's the work that matters. Some people call it *deep work*. It's the kind of work that adds value, increases skill, and is impossible to automate. It's the type of work you can get lost in. Like fixing a car, running an experiment, designing a chair, chasing a story, taking a master's degree, starting a business, or writing a book.

We are trying to get a new project off the ground. Some meaningful goal that subletts a room inside our minds and refuses to leave. It's what you daydream about when your rational self is caught off guard. We sit down and focus on this dream for a while, and what happens? Modern busyness sets in. The deep work is postponed.

And then there's distraction. Social media and the 24-hour

news cycle turned us into tiny gods instantly aware of any event anywhere in the world. There are over 7 billion people on Planet Earth; chances are, on a given day, one of them will do something horrific, or a new war begins, or an old war escalates. There's an earthquake somewhere, a fire, a flood. Catastrophe looms on our screens, and we wake up every day to an episode of the Old Testament—no wonder everyone's stressed.

There's more. We also have instant access to all the entertainment ever created. *Click*, here's all the music ever recorded, all the films, all the TV shows, all the books. Instantly and cheap (often free). Forget accelerating, the world entered hyperspeed.

Of course, digital technology has made life easier. Sure. But any new technology arrives with hidden costs. And hyper-advanced digital technology arrives with hyper-advanced hidden costs. That cost is your attention. It's not called the "attention economy" for nothing. And without attention, you can't focus. Focus is a particular type of attention that allows a person to learn, deepen an idea, develop a skill, and open the door for intuition. These days, focus is so rare you could invent a superhero whose power is the ability to focus.

A modern person's attention swings between hyperbusyness and hyperdistraction. When you sit down to work on something hard, you're not just battling the challenges of doing it; you're up against the forces of modern distraction and busyness. Against these foes, you're as powerless as a sand castle facing the rising tide.

Overwhelm sets in. We enter a *reactive* mode, putting out all the fires before we focus. Only when we clear out our obligations, we tell ourselves, can we focus on that project that matters.

But the fires of busyness can't be quenched, and the more you try, the higher the flames grow. Digital communication tools are a modern-day hydra, the mythical beast with multiplying heads. Slice one head off, and two rise in its place. Answer a message, and two follow-up messages emerge.

From a daily perspective, you're praised if you're quick. And when you're hard to reach, people get annoyed. If you unplug completely, people find you odd; believe me, I *know*. Unless you create work that adds value. In that case, you can disappear all you want.

That's the enigma of modern work. Society seems to value busyness. But it's an illusion. As another year passes, nobody cares how many meetings you attended, how many emails you answered, how many posts you liked, or how many updates you posted on social media. People value what you *do*. And so do you.

But the year ends, and restlessness fades. We return to the daily grind. We're too busy to be restless. And we wonder, how much faster must we run to cope with everyday demands?

Check mate

Keeping up with the pace of the modern world is as useless as trying to outrun a race car. Human beings are not fast. We're not fast at all. That's why we invented race cars, to go faster. And *that's* what we do well: we invent things.

Think about it: any computer can beat a person at chess. Chess is a closed problem that can be solved by processing information. And that's exactly what computers do, they process lots of information and fast. A computer can teach itself the rules of chess, play a billion games in a few minutes, develop the best strategy for any conceivable game state, and beat a grandmaster who spent his whole life practising chess moves. Check-mate humanity.

Or is it?

A computer can't **create** a game like Chess because creativity is not the product of information processing. Shakespeare did not have instant access to all the literature in the world, nor could he visit all the museums or concert halls. His world was smaller and slower, much slower than ours. And yet, here we are, still fascinated with Hamlet, Macbeth, and Romeo and Juliet.

If everyone is accelerating, slowness is scarce. And scarcity is valuable. Tasks a machine can do, a machine will do. So stop trying to keep up with computers; don't zip through your day like a robot. Instead, cultivate other skills. Slower skills that lead to creativity, intuition, and insight. Like writing.

Slow down

A Hare was taunting a Tortoise for being slow.
"Do you ever get anywhere?"
"Yes," said the Tortoise, "Race me, and I'll prove it."
The Hare laughed, the race was on, the Tortoise won.

Writing slows you down, and that's a good thing.

In the book "Hare Brain, Tortoise Mind", Professor Guy Claxton argues that the fast-paced environment of modern life **prevents** creativity from flourishing. Creative work is fragile. It requires regular periods of slow thinking and playful engagement for ideas to incubate and hatch.

Claxton uses the metaphor of the *hare brain* and *tortoise mind* to explain this idea. The hare brain represents the quick, reactive thinking that is seemingly prized in modern society. These days, we're like digital hares, hopping from distraction to distraction, from one urgent thing to the next.

The tortoise mind represents the slower, reflective thinking imperative for everything from scientific intuition to creative discovery. Claxton explains that work that's new and adds value depends on slowing down. Creative achievement requires time to develop without the pressure of immediate results. You can't rush intuition or insight, just like you can't rush the pattern of the tides. The tide of intuition ebbs and flows according to its own rules; it doesn't comply with the chronogram on a spreadsheet.

Writing requires a slower mindset. And a slower mindset is the first step towards control. The modern default state is reactive and fast. We're either too busy or distracted to notice where our attention goes. So, we gravitate towards daily demands and distractions like a moon doomed to follow its orbit.

Can we control the orbit of our attention?

Mindfulness

"There are these two young fish swimming along and they happen to meet an older fish swimming the other way, who nods at them and says "Morning, boys. How's the water?" And the two young fish swim on for a bit, and then eventually one of them looks over at the other and goes "What the hell is water?"

Not all those who wander are lost.

Bilbo Baggins,
from *The Lord of the Rings*

There's a reason why the first stage of the NODE method is the Note. Noticing what's **around** and **inside** you is hard when you're attracted to distractions like a kitten chasing laser beams. Noticing requires *mindfulness.*

Mindfulness is a mental state in which we turn our thoughts inward and focus on the present moment. It's about awareness and control. A mindful person is neither distracted nor busy; she **decides** where her attention will settle.

If you're mindful, you're not reacting. You're deciding what to focus on. Otherwise, you're like the two fish in the story, too "caught up in the moment" to realise they're swimming in water. But it gets harder. Focussing on what matters is insufficient because insights often arrive when we're not focussing at all.

Intuition shows up uninvited when we're neither focused nor distracted but **wandering**.

Mind-wandering

Mind-wandering is natural. It's our mental default setting. When we're not focused on the task at hand, our thoughts drift away, and the mind thinks about unrelated things. When we fall asleep, the mind wanders into dreams; when awake, we can steer into daydreams or let the mind go where it wills.

Mind-wandering allows your brain to make unexpected connections between ideas, leading to insights. We don't know how this happens, but we can let neuro-scientists worry about that. What matters is that mind-wandering is always running in the background. It kicks in when we don't focus and let the mind roam, like pressing "shuffle" on our mental playlist. You never know what the next thought will be.

It's easy to see why mind-wandering is vital for creativity. We wouldn't have stories about sudden insights without it. Sudden insights arrive while showering, jogging, driving, or any other moment when we're neither focusing nor distracted. Unless we willfully turn our attention somewhere, the mind is naturally wandering.

Not anymore, I'm afraid. Mind-wandering is no longer our default setting: People go grocery shopping while listening to podcasts, browse social media while waiting in line, answer emails during meetings, and play video games on the bus. The modern-day default setting is **distraction**.

Mind-wandering is not distraction. Distraction is when your attention is pulled towards some content. When distracted by external content, your brain must process the incoming information, and the mind-wandering mechanism shuts down. Mind-wandering doesn't have an object to lock on to. It's when your mind entertains itself.

Beyond boredom

Creative people know a secret: Boredom is just the first stop of the mind-wandering train. Hop in and ride beyond boredom into the following stops: imagination, inspiration, intuition, and insight. But you must first endure boredom. If you fight it and distract yourself, you fall off the train and return to the first stop. Most people can't tolerate boredom. Relearn how to tolerate it, and you're already ahead.

Your mind hates to be bored. So, she comes up with daydreams and absurd ideas. But you must leave it alone. If you feed your mind with information or entertainment, she'll start processing it, and you're off the wagon. But if you don't, your mind will start pitching ideas like a frenetic Hollywood producer.

21st Century superpowers

Modern society is set up to prevent creative work.

It sounds strange, but it's true. Everyone is in a reactive, distracted, fast-paced mindset that is a kryptonite for creativity. If you can avoid the busy/distracted kryptonite, you're a modern-day superhero.

Slow down and daydream: A slower, calmer mind is like a well-tended soil. Plant the seeds, water them, remove the weeds, take enough sunlight, and watch as your ideas grow. And be mindful of distractions like a farmer on the lookout for pests.

Focus without interruption, when you must. Focussed and uninterrupted efforts provide higher quality results, regardless of the task. Dedicating an hour daily to a meaningful project is better than fitting sporadic efforts in between daily tasks.

The NODE writing method trains you to slow down, daydream, and focus. Deep noting allows you to notice what's meaningful and filter information. When drafting a piece, you plug into your stream of consciousness. While editing, writing each sentence requires intense concentration, like a mathematician solving an equation or a swordsmith crafting a katana.

Whether you need to write to earn a degree or for personal or professional reasons, you are always reaching out to someone else. You're communicating with others and with yourself, too. Writing engages your mind completely.

If you reclaim your mind and focus when you need, in any circumstances; if you control your mind to let it daydream and wander intentionally; if you're mindful about your leisure and work time; if you notice what matters, filter and choose what goes into your head; if you are steadfast about what you want to achieve, you'll have a 21st century superpower. Controlling the mind is as powerful as flying around wearing a cape.

Writing can help you in that odyssey.

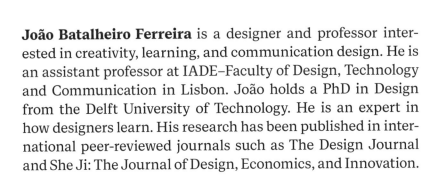

João Batalheiro Ferreira is a designer and professor interested in creativity, learning, and communication design. He is an assistant professor at IADE–Faculty of Design, Technology and Communication in Lisbon. João holds a PhD in Design from the Delft University of Technology. He is an expert in how designers learn. His research has been published in international peer-reviewed journals such as The Design Journal and She Ji: The Journal of Design, Economics, and Innovation.

References

"I write entirely to find out…": Didion, Joan. *Let me tell you what I mean*. New York: Alfred A. Knopf, 2021.

"It's not the writing part that's hard…": Pressfield, Steven. *The War of Art: Break Through the Blocks and Win Your Inner Creative Battles*. New York: Rugged Land, 2002.

"A coherent text is a designed object…": Pinker, Steven. *The sense of style: The thinking person's guide to writing in the 21st century*. London: Penguin Books, 2015.

Steve Jobs: "Design is how it works": Walker, Rob. *"The guts of a new machine."* The New York Times, November 30, 2003.

José Saramago: "If you can look, see…": Saramago, José. *Ensaio sobre a Cegueira*. Porto: Porto Editora, 2022.

"The power of the unaided mind…": Norman, Donald. *Things That Make Us Smart: Defending Human Attributes in the Age of the Machine*. Reading (MA): Addison-Wesley, 1993.

"The mind is for having ideas…": Allen, David. *Getting Things Done: The Art of Stree Free Productivity*. New York: Penguin Books, 2001.

"You can build a strong, sound structure…": McPhee, John. *Draft no. 4: On the Writing Process*. New York: Farrar, Straus and Giroux, 2017.

"Only thoughts that come by walking have any value.": Nietzsche, Friedrich. *Twilight of the Idols* Indianapolis: Hackett Publishing Company, 1997 (first published in 1889).

Productive meditation and Deep Work were proposed by:
Newport, Cal. *Deep Work: Rules for Focused Success in a Distracted World* New York: Grand Central Publishing, 2016.

"I begin to recognise myself…": DeLillo, Don. *Mao II*. New York: Penguin Books, 1991.

The idea of the "attentive ghost": Wolf, Maryanne. *Reader, Come Home*. Sydney: Harper Collins Publishers, 2018.

Writing as a conversation and clarity of presentation: Thomas, Francis-Noël and Turner, Mark. *Clear and Simple as the Truth: Writing Classic Prose*. Oxfordshire: Princeton University Press, 2011.

Academic writing should be clear: Sword, Helen. *Stylish Academic Writing*. Cambridge (MA): Harvard University Press, 2012.

The idea of "hitting the target" at the end of a sentence: Peter Clark, Roy. *How to Write Short: Word Craft for Fast Times*. New York: Little, Brown and Company, 2013.

"The potential people who…": Dawkins, Richard. Unweaving the Rainbow: Science, Delusin and the Appetite for Wonder. New York: Penguin Books, 1998.

"Join sentences with…": Moran, Joe. *First You Write a Sentence: The Elements of Reading, Writing … and Life*. Dublin: Penguin Random House, 2018.

Hare Brain and Tortoise Mind: Guy Claxton, Guy. Hare *Brain, Tortoise Mind:Why Intelligence Increases When You Think Less*. New York: HarperCollins, 1999.

The two fish story: Wallace, David. *This is water: Some thoughts, delivered on a significant occasion, about living a compassionate life*. London: Little, Brown Book Group, 2009.

"Not all those who wander are lost": Tolkien, John R. R. *The Lord of the Rings*. London: Harper Collins, 2007 (first published in 1954).